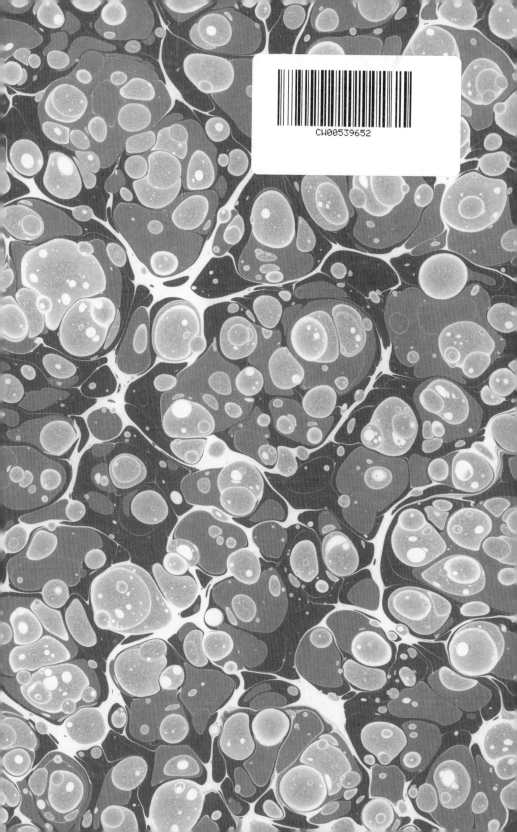

AN
IRISH
FOOD
STORY

To Marie Claire Digby, who took a leap of faith in me all those years ago and helped me hone my food writing skills, allowing me the creative freedom to investigate food in Ireland and Irish food. I am in part the food writer that you helped create. I shall always be in your debt.

AN IRISH FOOD STORY: 100 FOODS THAT MADE US

Jp McMahon

NINE BEAN ROWS

Contents

'We, in Ireland, have long memoires: the aromas from the kitchens of our childhood remain when many other things are forgotten. I hope that this little book will revive those memoires and pleasure to all who use it.'

THEODORA FITZGIBBON, *A Taste of Ireland* (1968)

Introduction

This book is about the story of Irish food and food in Ireland. They may seem like the same thing, but they're not.

'What is Irish food?' is the most common question I am asked, both at home and abroad. It's a difficult question for lots of reasons.

Ever since people arrived on this island 10,000 years ago, we have always been outward-looking. It's only recently that we started to think we were some sort of homogenous people who have always been here. Successive waves of migrants changed the Irish food landscape every so often, from the first hunter-gatherers and the first farmers to the Celts, Vikings and Normans, to name only a few. We were never just one thing, but rather always accumulating more ways of being that would eventually be called 'Irish'.

Once upon a time, we believed on the island of Ireland that we had no food story or cuisine of our own. We believed that any food culture that existed on this island came from elsewhere. Let me tell you a secret: Ireland is an island. Things on islands often come from elsewhere.

From oysters and seaweed to ginger and pies, no single ingredient can ever define Irish food. Though I would love our natural larder to take precedence, spices from the other side of the world are now just as Irish as our own indigenous ingredients. It may seem difficult to appreciate in an age of anxiety regarding migration, but the primary principle of food is migration. We cannot stop from food moving and crossing borders. Thus, any story of Irish food must consider what resides both inside and outside the island. As Dorothy Cashman observes in her PhD thesis (2016), 'all aspects of culinary history on the island [of Ireland] are worthy of the same attention: whether they are considered indigenous or otherwise.' We don't get to choose our food culture, although we can change it for the better. Our food culture chooses us, and it is constantly changing.

This book is a story of memory and desire, about what we had and what we wanted, about what we got and what we ate in our daily lives, from the very first settlers to those of us who now call Ireland home. It's about an oyster eaten straight from the sea to a pint of milk purchased in the supermarket, from wild mushrooms bought at the farmers' market to a late-night spice bag in the local chipper. It's about growing up and discovering food in Ireland – the good, the bad and the ugly – from Caffrey's Macaroon bars to Milleens cheese, from wild duck to Findus Crispy Pancakes, from pasta to potatoes.

It's also about what we *didn't* eat, about how we sometimes completely ignored the very foods that are right in front of us. It's about how we still struggle to assert our native food culture due to famine, self-doubt, colonialism and cultural dependency on those who had conquered us.

Food, as Máirtín Mac Con Iomaire (2018) observes, is part of Ireland's intangible cultural heritage. Just because we can't see it or touch it doesn't mean it's not there. Think of the many place names in the Irish language that have a food connotation, from *Léim an Bhradáin* (Leixlip) to *Rosmuc* (Rossmuck). The former refers to salmon (*bhradáin*), while the latter refers to pigs (*muc*). There is much to rediscover about our food culture through language, memory and artifact.

We Irish have long concerned ourselves with the religious and spiritual aspects of food in a broad sense but seem to have overlooked the pleasures in the ordinary, everyday act of eating. It is as rewarding to investigate the food around us, both its past and its present, as the many other cultural and creative forms that the Irish are well-known for, such as poetry, drama and literature.

All food has a story, but sometimes it's not the story we want it to have. Growing up, I was acutely aware of the paucity of our food culture. I knew we didn't value food as much as other nations like the French, Italians and Spanish. Young exchange students would speak proudly of their food (particularly the Spanish students who stayed with us during the summers), whereas we didn't speak of it at all. We just ate what we had. I recall my father eating dinner as quickly as possible to get back to the 'real' things in life, to what was important.

The older I got, the more this division seemed to grow. As I travelled to Spain and France in my late teens, I was amazed by their bread, their cured meats and hams, their cheese and much, much more. The gap between us and them seemed insurmountable. The Irish food story was spoken of with derision, if at all. Did we not have a food story?

When I asked my mother what foods she cooked for us when we were kids, a handwritten list arrived on a piece of cardboard a few days later. To my surprise, she had included a pork dish that I didn't recognise. Yes, we'd had grilled pork chops, but meatballs? I rang her and told her I didn't recall having ever eaten this dish as a child. She told me it was a Jamie Oliver recipe and that she must have made it for the other kids after I left home (I'm the second oldest).

What's interesting about this anecdote is that even in my own childhood, the things that my mother cooked were changing. Ireland was changing. From grilled pork chops to pork meatballs in tomato sauce. When I tell my two daughters this story, they laugh. Your life must have been so miserable, they say. Plain food, all the time. Was it miserable? I don't think so. But as American and British television crept into each Irish household, we began to leave behind the isolated standpoint that we had held since independence and grow more confident in who we are and what our unique food story means. At the turn of the 20th century, traditional Irish food encountered a new generation of food entrepreneurs, from chefs to farmers, from scholars to producers. The Irish food story had come home.

Irish food culture has come on in leaps and bounds in the last 40 years, but for many of us, Irish food still has no story and we don't know our own food identity. We don't know where we've come from and 'we don't know ourselves', as Fintan O'Toole remarks (2022*a*). We are still lost to some degree, blindly searching for evidence of our food story in a history mired in colonialism, famine and loss.

This book sits in that space where we find ourselves presently, with artisan food on one side and the industrial food system on the other, with independent coffee shops and international fast food outlets jostling for their share of the Irish food story. To find a way forward, we need to create an in-between space, a hybrid space that accommodates elements from both sides – a space where we can feed people in a way that recognises all aspects of our food culture.

We may want food to be one way or the other, but much as we try, we can't control the landscape of food. Food mirrors the migration of people. We imagine we are in control, but ultimately, we are not. To some degree, we need to just let food happen. Outside forces will always have to be contended with when we are creating a food culture. The high and the low, the good and the bad, the beautiful and the ugly: all our history is present in the food system that makes and unmakes us. Boxty, Wham Bars, oysters and a custard cream slice all have a place in Irish food culture, as this book demonstrates.

On a personal level, this book also encapsulates my life in food, all 47 years of it. Cooking professionally for 32 of those years (I took my first chef job at the age of 15) has given me a unique insight into how we, the Irish, see food in terms of its taste and cultural significance. Moreover, it is a manifesto of sorts to understand food as a cultural experience in Ireland, which is something we often fail to consider.

Even now, despite the last 20 years of an expanded Irish food renaissance, the word *culture* is not often used in terms of food. For many, culture resides firmly in the realm of art or sport, not food. We still have no Minister of Food (as a cultural experience) in Ireland, which says a lot about our general attitude to food. For many of us on this island, food is agriculture and production, nothing more. It is a commodity to be bought, sold and consumed when hungry. I hope this book places our food culture directly in your daily life and makes you think about how food fits into your own cultural experience, in much the same way you might feel when watching a

The high and the low, the good and the bad, the beautiful and the ugly: all our history is present in the food system that makes and unmakes us.

football game or visiting an art gallery or an historic Irish site. Food is as important as any subject we studied at school, from English to maths, woodwork to geography and history. We need to make food matter more. This book is a rallying cry to make food count in a quiet, revolutionary way.

Lastly, this book looks over the entire history of food in Ireland. Throughout this book, I often use the phrase 'food in Ireland' as opposed to 'Irish food', as I feel it encapsulates our sense of food over time. Often the phrase 'Irish food' limits our investigation of food on this island and evokes a sense of an 'Irish Ireland' cut off from Europe and the world. The Irish Ireland movement dominated cultural discourse in Ireland post-independence and claimed that Gaelic Ireland was the only Ireland (Moran 2006). Gaelic Ireland is deeply important, but it is not the only 'Ireland'. From before the Gaelic order until after its collapse, there are many Irelands to uncover and therefore many foodways to discover. The relationship between food in Ireland and Irish food is thus a fluid one. The 'conservative's vision of the nation's life' of food can often end in chauvinism, bigotry and racism (Brown 2004: 53).

People (Irish and otherwise) have been in Ireland for over 10,000 years and they have eaten every day since then. As the late Jock Zonfrillo once told me, 'Where there are people, there is food, and where there is food, there is culture. You don't just get by.' The people on the island of Ireland are a culmination of at least 10,000 years of food culture, both good and bad, feast and famine. Let's explore it and celebrate it together. Only then can we take our place alongside the other great food nations of the world.

How to use this book

This book is both a standalone snapshot of the history and vicissitudes of Irish food and food in Ireland and a companion to the two previous books on Irish food that I have written – *The Irish Cookbook* (2020) and *An Alphabet of Aniar: Notes for a New Irish Cuisine* (2022) – and my weekly columns in the *Irish Times* that ran from 2015 to 2022.

At times, it is deeply personal. Other times, it is much more analytic, historical and philosophical, probing the nuances of what the phrase 'Irish food' might mean. In all, it's a book to enjoy for pleasure as well as a book to encourage you to think seriously and critically about food in Ireland.

This book can be read from start to finish or you can open it at random and read a section, then pop over to another section. The list is not conclusive or exhaustive; I'm sure many readers will remember foods that made up their experience of Irish food and food in Ireland that aren't included here.

Food in any country is never exhaustive. We can never finish mining the past for new ways of looking at things, just as we can't stop the future from changing our present ways. The food of Ireland is in flux. I hope this book captures the drama – the good, the bad, the beautiful – and the wonderous aspects of Irish food and food in Ireland over the millennia that have preceded us.

○○I

Angel Delight

I think the very words *Angel Delight* would make an Irish person over a certain age swoon. How can a reconstituted powder turned into mousse with only the addition of milk form such an important part of my Irish childhood? Perhaps my love of mousse can be traced back to watching my mother whisk up this powder with the electric mixer. It was a regular dessert in my family and often appeared from the fridge at the many birthday parties that took place in our house.

Angel Delight goes all the way back to 1967. The product slumped in terms of popularity in the 1980s, but by 2015, it was named Britain's favourite dessert (Sayid 2015). While Britain is not Ireland, we like many of the same things, so I would imagine it was a thumbs-ups from the Irish as well. We often imagine our nearest neighbours are very different than ourselves, due in no small part to the long legacy of colonialism, but we share similar tastes when it comes down to the everyday things.

In the 194th Royal Hibernian Academy of Arts show in 2024, the Irish artist Debbie Godsell included a package of Angel Delight in the centre of her food print *Harvest Thanksgiving* (2023). The beautiful still-life print, which includes many other foodstuffs, from ducks and mouldy bread to tins of Heinz soup and turnips, all positioned on an elaborately covered table, seems to take an ironic attitude towards the meeting of natural and processed foodstuffs.

I would be afraid to try Angel Delight now, as I don't want to ruin my precious memories of the past, when licking the bowl was a treat that made my day.

002

Apples

In *Sláinte: The Complete Guide to Irish Craft Beer and Cider*, Hennessy and Jensen (2014: 66) state, 'Apples have been grown in Ireland for at least 3,000 years. They feature in the Ulster legends and are mentioned in Irish literature as far back as the 7th century. St Patrick is even said to have planted a number of apple trees in Ireland.'

In *The Irish Apple: History and Myth*, Lamb and Hayes (2012) write, 'No other tree appears so frequently as the apple in early Irish documents. Apples appear in the sagas, in the voyages, in place-name lore, in the lives of the saints and in the Fenian tales. Records of apples appear in the annals.'

You only need to look at how many Irish place names have the word *úll* ('apple') in them to see how important the apple was in the Irish food culture: Aghowle, Co. Wicklow (from *Achadhadhla*, 'The Field of the Apple Trees'); Ballyhooly, Co. Cork (from *Baile Átha hÚlla*, 'Pass of the Ford of the Apple Trees'); Cappaghnanool, Co. Galway (from *Ceapach na n-ubhal*, 'Plot of the Apples'); Clonoutly, Co. Tipperary (from *Cluain Ula*, 'Meadow of the Apple Trees'); Oola, Co. Limerick (from *Úlla*, 'Apple'); and Oulart, Co. Wexford (from An *tAbhallort*, 'The Orchard'), to name just a few (Hennessy and Jensen 2014).

There are currently 180 varieties of apple seeds available through the Irish Seed Savers Association, yet we import 95% of our apples. Of those, 80% come from only five varieties. Why is this? Given that we even have apples with Protected Geographical Indication (PGI) status (Armagh Bramley apples were awarded PGI status in 2012), why don't we pay more attention to our native apples in Ireland?

Another crazy fact is that the apple that you just purchased from the supermarket could be up to a year old. I'm old enough to remember when you could still pick an apple from a tree in autumn and eat it; that was only 30 years ago. My friend's grandmother had a few apple trees in her garden. We used to pick a few and eat them before wandering into the fields, with grass that grew nearly as high as us, looking for mischief and adventure in an old house a few fields away.

Apple tarts, crumbles and pies

Sweet apple pies, as Darina Allen (1995) observes, were a staple in Irish homes of the 20th century, with recipes passed down from mother to daughter. Everyone's mother in my generation made apple tarts – they were a mainstay of my childhood. While travelling up and down to Cork I still see homemade apple tarts for sale in the shops, but I don't think they are part of our daily consciousness anymore. Does anyone still yearn for a warm apple tart with freshly whipped cream?

Before the advent of modern ovens, the pies would have been cooked in a bastible, like soda bread. Many medieval apple pies were heavily spiced with cinnamon, nutmeg and ginger, particularly in wealthy households, so they would have tasted very different to the ones your mother or granny may have made. In the cooking classes in Aniar, I get students to make Richard Corrigan's apple tart. It's like an apple tart on steroids, with whiskey, sultanas, lemon zest and caramelised brown sugar.

Let's not forget apple crumbles and pies. As with so many traditional dishes in Ireland, there are a multitude of variations, especially when other fruit is in season, such as apple and blackberry or apple and rhubarb. Like wild fruit jams, apple always seems to get in there to bulk everything up.

Though we don't know if they were making tarts, blackberries and apples are mentioned in the 12th-century text *The Colloquy of the Ancients* (*Agallamh na Seanórach*), which features the legendary Fionn Mac Cumhaill.

Black apple butter

Black apple butter is neither a butter nor a fermented product. It's a kind of apple preserve or chutney made with apples, sugar, cider and spices, though it can also include brandy and treacle. The process is said to date back to the medieval period in Ireland and most likely came from Europe with the Normans.

Black apple butter (as well as other fruit butters, such as damson butter) was traditionally made to preserve autumn fruit and was served with cheese and cold meats. Nowadays, black apple butter is a popular condiment. In Aniar, we make a variation of it by cooking apples in a rice cooker for six to eight weeks (yes, weeks) at a very low temperature until they blacken. This concentrates the sugar and makes a lovely purée that works well with wild game, such as wood pigeon.

Today, black apple butter made in Co. Armagh has EU Protected Geographical Indication (PGI) status. Armagh in Northern Ireland has long been known as the 'Orchard County' of Ireland and is famous for cider-making and other apple derivates, from juice to vinegars and treacle. Armagh has over 4,000 acres of orchards and the apple is said to have been in the county for over 3,000 years, so if you're taking a trip to Armagh, be sure to experience the apple there.

○○3

Bananas

In my ongoing search for Irish food – or rather, experiences of food in Ireland – what we ate in the past and how that sits with what we consider to be within the bounds of our food culture never ceases to amaze me. From seal-hunting on the Blasket Islands to bananas cooked in cabbage leaves in Kylemore Abbey, the diversity of the experience of food on this island over the centuries is outstanding. Why do we continually reduce our cultural experience of food to the humble potato and a bowl of Irish stew? If you peel back the layers, you'll unearth a diverse richness that will go beyond your expectations.

It's incredible to think that bananas, pineapples and figs grew in Connemara in the 19th century. The ingenious heating system for the glasshouses in Kylemore produced exotic fruit that would have been highly unusual for the time and place.

Of course, not everyone had access to these foods. Pineapple plants arrived in England around 1719 and gradually made their way to the greenhouses (called pineries) in England and Ireland. They were extremely rare and expensive to maintain. People would put pineapples on display as opposed to eating them as they signified such wealth. People even used to rent pineapples to demonstrate their affluence.

But back to bananas. Bananas cooked with cabbage seems like a bizarre configuration, even in the 19th century, but the combination does exist and is particular to Caribbean cooking. Green (under-ripe) bananas, which have a lower sugar content and are starchier than ripe bananas, were used so that they would hold up to the savoury cooking. Green bananas are generally simmered in their skins until tender, then served with salted fish or pork. Thinking of our own tradition of salted ling, I wonder if this Jamaican influence somehow wound its way to Kylemore in the latter half of the 19th century.

004

Barley

Barley first came to Ireland with Neolithic farmers, most likely from Scotland, where it was the primary Neolithic grain (Smyth and Evershed 2015). Though not the dominant crop (it was planted alongside emmer, einkorn, common wheat and flax), naked and hulled barley was an important food source for these early Irish farmers, though we know little about how it was produced and cultivated or what foods were made with it (McClatchie et al. 2014). Charred barley from the period indicates its presence but not its use.

Barley beer was probably one of the first alcoholic drinks developed by Neolithic peoples in the Fertile Crescent, where it was also used as a currency (Pellechia 2006). According to Pliny the Elder in his *Natural History*, barley was dried and roasted and made into a porridge, so we can assume a similar method of consumption also occurred in Ireland.

Bizarrely, at present no barley is produced in Ireland for human consumption (unless you count the many tonnes that get turned into whiskey, ales, beers and stouts). A lot of barley gets eaten by the cows, and we do have a lot of cows. This is strange considering we have such a long history of using barley as food in Ireland. Barley grew better than wheat here because of our inclement climate. Though you can pick up naked barley for making your own flour, a pack of pearl barley in the supermarket here is usually French or Spanish.

Barley bread has a rich history in Ireland, though I don't know of anyone making it now. Barley bread, watercress and fresh or pickled fish (often salmon or trout) would have been a medieval staple for many monks in Early Christian Ireland.

There are many other possibilities nowadays when it comes to barley, from 'risottos' and flavouring bread or crackers with barley flour to using it to make koji to produce Irish miso.

○○5
Barmbrack

Barmbrack is a cake that was traditionally eaten at Halloween. Barmbrack is the most famous brack but there are many others, such as tea brack and apple brack. Theodora FitzGibbon (1983) observes that there are two types of brack: one made with yeast and the other with baking powder.

Brack is less popular today than it was in the past, though you still see brack in shops all year round. Baker Graham Herterich is putting modern twists on this Irish classic in his bakery in Rialto, Dublin, with flavour combinations such as Earl Grey, cranberry and orange, or lemon, ginger and pistachio.

Whether it's called barmbrack or barnbrack is a food history conundrum. Food historian Regina Sexton has mulled over the question, observing that 'the Battle of the Barners and Barmers' of 1927 'can be viewed as a divide between the practices of home and commercial bakers. But on another level, it played out against a backdrop of language where familiarity, or otherwise, with Ulster Gaelic was seen as a decisive means of settling the debate on the "correct" naming of the barn/barm brack' (Sexton 2023).

In the Irish language, it's called *bairín breac*. The Irish word *bairín* translates as 'loaf' and *breac* translates as 'speckled' (due to the raisins). I'm not sure 'speckled loaf' has the same ring to it.

Before the advent of bicarbonate of soda or baking powder, brack would have been made with barm, the froth on the fermenting malt liquor for beer. The bread is sweet, but not as sweet as a cake. It is often served with butter and tea.

Traditionally, objects such as a pea, a stick, a rag of cloth, a coin, a ring and a bean would be placed in the bread at Halloween. The finder of each object would have their fortune told through each object. The pea signified that the person would not marry that year; the stick meant that the finder would have an unhappy marriage or continually be in arguments or disputes with others; the rag of cloth cast bad luck or poverty on its victim; the coin (originally a six-penny piece) purportedly brought good fortune; the ring meant marriage within the year; and the bean signified future happiness without money. Nowadays, some commercially made barmbrack contains a ring, though most other objects have faded from use (probably because they are a choking hazard!).

In *Dubliners* by James Joyce (2000), there is a reference to barmbrack in the story 'Clay': 'The fire was nice and bright and on one of the side-tables were four very big barmbracks. These barmbracks seemed uncut; but if you went closer you would see that they had been cut into long thick even slices and were ready to be handed round at tea.'

Lady Gregory, one of the founders of the Abbey Theatre in Dublin, used to bring tea brack up from her estate in Coole, Co. Galway when she attended rehearsals. It is said the actors ate it with 'contempt', though there was never a morsel left (the fact that it was doused in brandy may have helped). Called a 'Gort Cake', the brack was full of 'spice, raisins and currants' (O'Casey 1980*b*: 120).

006

Beef

In Ireland, 'cattle is king' – that is, according to the New York consultancy firm Stacy May, which published a report on Ireland in 1952 (O'Toole 2022*b*).

It's hard to imagine the Irish food story without cows, but before farming began around 4000 BC, there was not a single cow in the land. It's said that the English turned Ireland into a grazing ground for cattle, but the Gaelic economy was measured in cattle. In fact, the entire Gaelic order was based on pastoralism, as historian Jane Ohlmeyer observes in her book *Making Empire: Ireland, Imperialism and the Early Modern World* (2023). *The Book of the Dun Cow* (*Lebor na hUidre*), written on vellum in the 12th century, testifies to the sacred importance of the cow in Gaelic culture.

Cattle raids were frequent in Old Ireland because cattle were how you showed your wealth – the size of one's herd was an indication of power, so numbers mattered. Due to the high status of the cow, dairy consumption took precedence over eating beef (Sexton 1998).

Many Irish words, such as *bóthar* ('road'), derive from the fact that 'a road was defined in width by the length and breadth of a cow (*bó*). In Irish, the name for Westport in County Mayo is "*Cathair na Mart*", which means "the city of the beef"' (Mac Con Iomaire and Óg Gallagher, 2011).

Cattle raids take place in much early Irish literature, such as *The Cattle Raid of Cooley* (written around the 12th century, but probably from an older oral tradition) and in *The Annals of Ulster* (431–1540 AD). 'I never saw so many cows in one place in all my life', says Mabel in Brian Friel's play *Making History* (1989), a play about the last stand of the old Gaelic order in Ulster before the British finally occupied the whole island.

Some even argue that beef farming contributed to the Famine (*An Gorta Mór* – The Great Hunger) because all the good land was used for cattle, thus leaving Irish farmers little choice other than growing potatoes.

The image of Irish food around the world is often associated with beef, not least because we export over 90% of the beef produced in this country. This comes at great expense to many of our other products. So what can we do to change this story? Change will be difficult, as we have been exporting beef from Ireland in large amounts since at least the 17th century (Truxes 1988).

Our diet turned inwards in the Neolithic period, away from the sea and towards the land, but this does not mean we have to persist in creating a veritable monoculture based around beef. Meanwhile, generations of Irish people have been reared on beef (and pork to a lesser extent), while fish and vegetables feature lower down the list. We need to invert this schema for the next generation. We need to focus on smaller heritage varieties of beef, particularly ones like Dexter, which originated in the 18th century in Co. Kerry. Using retired dairy cattle as beef, a practice that is as old as farming itself, is a more sustainable and regenerative form of beef farming that also needs to be embraced in Ireland.

Beef & Guinness stew

This stew was the bane of my life when I first started cooking in Galway in the late 1990s, when beef and Guinness stew and chicken à la king were the two most popular 'wet' dishes ordered for outdoor catering. Another thing that irked me about this dish was that it was always in the top five 'Irish' dishes people (particularly Americans) named when asked to list a few dishes associated with Irish cuisine.

My ire has lessened in the last few years, but I still love telling people that this dish is probably only a couple hundred years old. (Compare this to shellfish and seaweed, which have been eaten here for 10,000 years.) Beef and Guinness stew only emerged in the 19th century (initially it was made with any stout or even any beer) and has gained popularity ever since as being representative of Irish food.

Beef Wellington (Wellington steak)

Beef Wellington is a fillet of beef that is coated in a cooked mushroom paste called a duxelles, then wrapped in pancakes and puff pastry.

It is purportedly named after Arthur Wellesley, the 1st Duke of Wellington, who was born in Dublin in 1769. I say purportedly as there is no direct evidence that connects the dish to the man. FitzGibbon remarks that this beef dish was 'said to be a favourite of the Duke of Wellington' (1983: 113), but we may never know how this dish came to be called after an Irishman who was more famous for being English.

In Ireland, beef Wellington was often called Wellington steak. The dish was also known in France, where it was called *filet de boeuf en croûte* (P.B. Stevens 1998: 96).

Writing in *The New York Times Food Encyclopedia* (1985), Craig Claiborne observed, 'I am persuaded that beef Wellington is of Irish origin. In *Irish Traditional Food*, Theodora FitzGibbon offers a recipe for *Steig* Wellington, using the Irish spelling for steak.'

The oldest known reference to beef Wellington is from the *Los Angeles Times* in 1903; the first occurrence of the dish recorded in the *Oxford English Dictionary* is a quotation from a 1939 New York food guide that includes 'Tenderloin of Beef Wellington'; and its first entry in an American cookbook is from the 1940s. There are no 19th-century references to the dish in England or in Ireland, even though beef wrapped in pastry was a common-enough practice going back to the 18th century. So did this dish come back to us via America?

In her cookbook *Great British Cooking: A Well-Kept Secret* (1981), Jane Garmey includes beef Wellington, observing that the recipe's origins are a mystery. We may never know how this popular American dish of the 1960s was named (or rather, renamed), but this story demonstrates how food often travels and returns in a different guise. A dish such as this gets to the kernel of the problem of Irish food, or rather, the problem of an 'Irish' food story.

Corned beef

The first recorded mention of corned (or rather, salted) beef dates to the 12th century in the poem *The Vision of MacConglinne*. In later centuries, Irish merchants who traded with their French counterparts imported salt to Cork and Waterford to make this unique product.

Cork was the centre for corned beef production from the 17th to the 19th century. Unfortunately, it was not the people of Ireland who got

This story demonstrates how food often travels and returns in a different guise. A dish such as beef Wellington gets to the kernel of the problem of Irish food, or rather, the problem of an 'Irish' food story.

to eat this tasty treat (or at least, not most of them); it was destined for the British Empire. As more new books emerge on British imperial food policy, such as *Making Empire: Ireland, Imperialism and the Early Modern World* by Jane Ohlmeyer (2023), it is shocking to realise how much food left Ireland during the Famine in the service of the Empire.

Irish corned beef was used and traded extensively from the 17th century to the mid-19th century for British civilian consumption and as provisions for the British naval fleets, as its preserved qualities (corns were large salt crystals) made it suitable for long ship journeys. During that period, it was shipped all over the world, including to the West Indies to feed the slave populations working in the plantations there.

With the advent of canning, corned beef would keep even longer and became a staple food during World War One. Eating canned corned beef on the battlefield in France was a common occurrence before going over the top for many an Englishman and Irishman.

Corned beef and cabbage is regularly associated with the Irish, particularly by Americans. This is supposedly due to the fact that corned beef was more widely available than pork Stateside in kosher butchers. However, Colman Andrews, in his book *The Country Cooking of Ireland* (2009), disputes this.

Bacon and cabbage was more popular in Ireland than corned beef and cabbage, likely due to the high cost of beef. For Bríd Mahon (1991: 57), corned beef 'served with green cabbage and floury potatoes' was a common dish for special occasions, such as at Halloween and Christmas. According to Mahon, it is this tradition that travelled with the many emigrants who left Ireland in the 18th and 19th centuries. Thus, an Irish-American dish became associated with Ireland due to the diaspora. This case of food migration is not unique and demonstrates the difficulties when we go in search of authenticity in national cuisines.

Spiced beef

Spiced beef is a variation of corned beef. Historically, spices may have been introduced to offset the salty flavour or to hide a putrid smell, but it's more likely that they were a way of adding an exotic touch to a cheaper cut. For many, traditional Irish food is an unspiced affair. But this is not altogether true. In modern times the addition of pink salt (potassium nitrate) would have helped preserve the beef, but now it's added to give the beef its distinctive pink colour after cooking.

Spiced beef is popular in the South of Ireland, especially Cork, but it is also widely eaten at Christmastime around the country, especially on St Stephen's Day. Spiced beef cooked in Guinness at Christmas offers a culinary insight into faded past traditions in Ireland. In Joyce's last short story in *Dubliners* (2000), 'The Dead', set on 6 January 1904, a 'round of spiced beef' sits nobly on the table alongside goose, ham and many other foodstuffs associated with an Irish Edwardian Christmas: 'While Gabriel and Miss Daly exchanged plates of goose and plates of ham and spiced beef Lily went from guest to guest with a dish of hot floury potatoes wrapped in a white napkin.'

Nowadays, spiced beef is available all year round in butchers and even some supermarkets.

007

Bird's Custard

Little did Alfred Bird know when he made his first powdered custard (because his wife was allergic to eggs) in 1837 that he would transform the lives of millions, giving 'instant' custard to many who might never have seen it before. Nowadays, the problem is getting someone to make custard from scratch.

Bird's custard, along with Angel Delight, caused a revolution in Irish homes. No longer did 'housewives' have to make homemade custard. Now you could just warm milk and add this yellow powder.

We always had Bird's custard in our house. Ironically, I think it was a badge of honour. It was a message to those who made things from scratch: look at us, look how modern we are. The first time I made real custard as a chef, it was both an emotional and alchemic process: I was simply amazed.

My mum's sherry trifle was always made with Bird's custard. For a quick dessert, Bird's custard would be served with broken biscuits and jelly that was also made from a packet. Custard and jelly. How modern indeed.

As well as Bird's custard, many Irish people fondly remember Bird's Dream Topping, which was a cream substitute. A little like Angel Delight, all you have to do is add the powder to milk and whip it. (I'm not sure what's wrong with simply whipping cream instead.) What is it about instant powdered desserts that we seem to gravitate towards?

oo8
Black & white pudding

Black pudding is a sausage made from pig's blood, pork fat, spices and oats. Black pudding used to be made by the women on the farm and sold at local markets as a way of supplementing the farm income.

There are many different regional recipes around the country – for example, in Cork they would use sheep's blood to make a pudding called drisheen. It was often a communal activity, with Mahon (1991: 59) remarking that 'every single person who helped in the salting was given some of the pork to take home with them.'

Nowadays, most black pudding is made from dried pig's blood. It doesn't have the same texture or flavour as pudding made with fresh blood, but most butchers have made the switch due to changes in the industry from the 1960s onwards. It's difficult now to source fresh pig's blood. Inch House in Co. Mayo, McCarthy's of Kanturk in Co. Cork and Hugh Maguire in Co. Meath still make black pudding with fresh blood. Meanwhile, Kelly's Butchers are famous for their *putóg*, which is a black pudding made in the traditional manner. As well as being made with ox or sausage casings, recipes exist that bake the mixture in a loaf pan. One such recipe is included in Florence Irwin's book *The Cookin' Woman: Irish Country Recipes* (1949: 76). I love the beginning of the method: 'The blood is caught in a basin at the killing of the pig. Stir until almost cold.' They don't write recipes like they used to.

White pudding is similar to black pudding, save for the absence of blood. It originated in Ireland in the Middle Ages. There are many extant recipes from the 16th to the 18th century, which contain a variety of fillings, from almonds to rice and eggs. Most Irish white pudding contains oats, lard and onions with various spices, such as allspice, white pepper, nutmeg and mace. Tansy was traditionally used to flavour the pudding, though now thyme is generally used instead. Like black pudding, it can be made either as a sausage or in a loaf.

oo9
Bread

According to food historian Regina Sexton (1998), 'No matter how hard you try, you can't but fall victim to Ireland's impressive bread tradition.' There is a long history of baking in Ireland from at least the 7th century. A text from that time, *Cáin Íarraith* ('Law of the Fosterage Fee'), stipulated that foster parents were legally obliged to teach the skill of baking, namely 'flour sieving, kneading, and baking' to young girls (Sexton 1998: 84). From that point on, baking became indelibly linked to the Irish psyche.

Grains arrived in Ireland with Neolithic farmers. Emmer, barley, wheat and oats all became a staple part of the diet from around 3000 BC onwards. Legend tells us that a woman invented sourdough when she left a little of the remaining dough in her bowl and mixed fresh dough with it. Barm (the liquid obtained from making beer) was also used to get bread to rise (*see also* 'Barmbrack', page 14). Two other interesting methods that Bríd Mahon (1991) writes of were the use of sowans (the juice of fermented oat husks) and sour potato water. The recent emergence of fermented potato bread in Ireland, such as that made by Ciaran Sweeney at The Olde Glen in Donegal, appears to have truly ancient Irish origins.

It would be wrong to see bread as a staple product of Irish cooking over time because every invading group modified the existing bread. Furthermore, wheat was difficult to grow in Ireland because of the weather. In one sense, this is why our bread tradition comes and goes over the centuries. One traveller to Ireland in the 18th century noted that bread from the South was usually made with oats, but in the Midlands, it would be made with rye and wheat. An old Irish proverb stated:

Rye bread will do you good,
Barley bread will do you no harm.
Wheaten bread will sweeten your blood,
Oaten bread will strengthen your arm.

While barley bread was associated with the fasting monks of the 7th and 8th centuries (barley bread in the Middle Ages must have taken the teeth out of the monks who ate it), soft wheaten cakes came with the Normans, who loved their feasts and always included luxurious spiced breads (*see also* 'Wheat', page 185).

The oven also arrived with the Normans, which did much to change the nature of bread-making in Ireland. It became more refined, if only for the aristocratic classes; for most, bread remained a simple affair, cooked on a griddle pan over an open fire. There were two bread traditions in Ireland – one for the rich and one for the poor – until the arrival of the middle class in the 19th century. This tradition is mirrored in European history, where barley and rye bread was eaten by the peasant class, while refined wheat products were consumed by the upper classes (McGee 2004).

The future is bright for Irish bread-making, with many new bakeries opening all around the country. Bread 41, run by Eoin Cluskey, is one such bakery, which is returning heritage and craft to baking. Producers are also planting different varieties of grain and wheat in order to reclaim our bread heritage. For example, Little Mill in Co. Kilkenny is the only commercial stone-ground mill in Ireland producing wholemeal flour from Irish wheat.

Batch loaf

A batch loaf is a tall loaf of bread with a dark crust on the top and bottom. There is no crust on the sides because the unbaked loaves are placed side by side in batches (hence the name) when rising. The loaves are baked together, then torn into individual loaves once baked.

Bread & butter pudding

Bread and butter pudding appears in many Irish cookbooks of the last 100 years, from Maura Laverty and Monica Sheridan to Darina Allen. It's defined as a British dessert, but this is probably because it originated in England and played a part in feeding the Anglo-Irish aristocracy in the Big Houses.

Bread and butter pudding encapsulates the no-waste philosophy of much traditional Irish cooking. Regina Sexton observes that in Cork during the 1920s to the 1940s, children would bring the stale bread from their house to the bakeries to encourage the bakers to make the pudding (Allen 1995: 297).

Bread and butter pudding is made by layering slices of leftover buttered bread, scattered with raisins, in an oven dish, then pouring an egg custard over it. Seasoning usually includes spices such as nutmeg, cinnamon, vanilla and often lemon or orange peel. Several recipes include a dash of brandy, whiskey or sweet sherry in the custard.

One of the earliest published recipes for a bread and butter pudding is found in Eliza Smith's *The Compleat Housewife* (2012):

> Take a two penny loaf, and a pound of fresh butter; spread it in very thin slices, as to eat; cut them off as you spread them, and stone half a pound of raisins, and wash a pound of currants; then put puff-paste at the bottom of a dish, and lay a row of your bread and butter, and strew a handful of currants, a few raisins, and some little bits of butter, and do so till your dish is full; then boil three pints of cream and thicken it when cold with the yolks of ten eggs, a grated nutmeg, a little salt, near half a pound of sugar, and some orange flower-water; pour this in just as the pudding is going into the oven.

Though published in London in 1727, Smith's book was the first cookbook to be published in the 13 colonies of America when it was printed in Williamsburg, Virginia, in 1742. It brought bread and butter pudding Stateside.

Farl/fadge

Some, particularly people from Ulster, may say it's blasphemous to put these two types of 'bread' under the same heading. Indeed, as well as being made with bread soda (soda farl), they can also be made with potato (potato farl). Is it a cake or a bread? Or a kind of large scone? We do like different words for the same thing in Ireland. It can get quite confusing.

Farls were traditionally shaped in a round loaf, then cut into quarters and cooked on a cast iron griddle pan over an open fire. Apple treacle was often added to make a sweet version. Farls were traditionally fried in pork fat to accompany an Ulster fry.

A fadge seems to always have potato included in it and rarely used a raising agent (although there are many regional variations). Butter or bacon fat was whipped together with leftover mashed potatoes and some flour, then fried. A fadge could be flat or shaped into bread and cut into four (like a farl). A fadge could also be served in the shape of a pancake. So for all intents and purposes, a fadge is a potato cake by another name.

Fried bread

I don't know if people still eat fried bread, but it was a staple of my childhood. It's simply bread fried in beef dripping or lard. My mother would have it with her breakfast on the weekend.

In her book *The Cookin' Woman*, Florence Irwin (1949: 145) includes a good observation in favour of fried bread: 'Wheaten or soda bread fried in the pan almost go with bacon and eggs without saying'. For Irwin, after the eggs and bacon are cooked, a little extra dripping could be added to the pan. Perhaps the modern toaster brought an end to this great tradition or perhaps it was our unfounded fear of frying with animal fats. The next time you're having a fry for your full Irish breakfast with bacon and eggs, why not indulge with a piece of fried bread too?

Sliced pan

The advent of industrially made white bread in the 19th century brought both good and bad things to the state of Ireland. On the positive side, the bread was fortified with vitamins to ensure a healthier population, especially children. The same was done to breakfast cereals. On the downside, it reduced the number of people baking bread themselves. As 'white baker's bread' was seen as superior, it ended up replacing soda bread in people's daily diets (Sexton 1998: 85). Ironically, homemade breads were looked down on for generations afterwards.

With the invention of the Chorleywood process, white baker's bread could be made much faster than a traditional loaf, much to the detriment of our stomachs, since the bread isn't given enough time to ferment. Bread made this way also has many more ingredients, from stabilisers to modifiers and preservatives. Think, for example,

During the late 19th and early 20th centuries, the smell of freshly baked brown soda bread became synonymous with the rural Irish kitchen. This tradition has travelled to America and beyond and epitomises the Irish food experience and its story.

of a loaf of soda bread, which has only four ingredients: flour, water or buttermilk, salt and the raising agent. Bread made with the Chorleywood process has over 24 ingredients.

However, white sliced pan will always triumph any childhood memory of bread in my mind. From ham and cheese sandwiches to egg and mayonnaise with chives or watercress (always good at funerals), crisp sandwiches or even sugar sandwiches, these soft white pillows of dough will forever transport me back to simpler times.

Soda bread

Most people today associate soda bread with Ireland, but it's not as old as you might think. Though we have been making bread for at least 1,000 years in Ireland, bicarbonate of soda (as a leavening agent) was only invented in the 19th century.

Despite it being a new-enough tradition (less than 200 years old), the advent of bicarbonate of soda made it possible for people without access to ovens to make their own bread daily. Soda bread was traditionally made in a bastible (a cast iron pot) that would hang over the fire in the middle of the hearth. During the late 19th and early 20th centuries, the smell of freshly baked brown soda bread became synonymous with the rural Irish kitchen. This tradition has travelled to America and beyond and epitomises the Irish food experience and its story.

My grandma made soda bread every second or third day, and as I grew older, I used to make it for her in the mornings when I stayed with her. It is this act of baking soda bread that I turn to when I try to untangle my own food origins.

Vienna bread

Words are important, especially for food. Going to the shop to buy a loaf of Vienna bread felt more like a mission abroad. I wasn't just going to buy bread; I may as well have been on my way to Vienna. My mother liked a poppy seed Vienna loaf, especially at breakfast. I have memories of these freshly baked loaves sitting in the Elite bakery on the main street of Maynooth, Co. Kildare.

Traditionally, Vienna bread, in contrast to French bread, has a chewy, coarse texture. This may have been because Vienna bread was originally made with different wheat than French baguettes. Interestingly, Vienna bakers, specifically August Zang, are credited with injecting steam into the baking process in the 19th century, which subsequently influenced French, and thus Irish, bakers throughout the 20th century.

Waterford blaa

The Waterford blaa is another tale of Irish food migration. The fact that we are an island means many peoples have come from elsewhere and have brought traces of their food culture with them. When the French Huguenots fled France because of persecution in the 16th century, they settled in Waterford. It is said they introduced the method for making this bread roll by importing white flour from France to Ireland.

As Darina Allen (1995: 248) observes, the blaa began its life as a by-product of making larger loaves of bread. The smaller pieces that were left over were shaped into rolls and baked, then 'often given away for free or bartered for another product.'

A poem written in the 1950s by Eddie Wymberry celebrates this local bread:

> *A Blaa with two a's is made with fresh dough*
> *About the size of a saucer, that's the right size you know:*
> *But where did they come from, did they happen by chance*
> *No, the Huguenots brought them from France.*

The roll now has EU Protected Geographical Indication (PGI) status. Walsh's bakery is continuing the tradition of making Waterford blaa and supplies them nationwide. They're great for a rasher (bacon) sandwich loaded with good country butter – Denny, the famous Irish makers of sausages and bacon, was also based in Waterford, so rashers and sausages generally filled the blaa there.

Yellow bread

Cornmeal (maize) arrived in Ireland during the Famine to relieve the starving population. The Irish called it 'Indian meal' and made a yellow bread referred to locally as 'yalla male' bread.

The Irish novelist and food writer Maura Laverty writes of her grandmother making corn cakes in the ashes of the fire in 1920. The scene that she paints in her novel *Never No More*, which was originally published in 1942, speaks of the ways in which bread was cooked over a traditional open hearth in Ireland in the 1920s:

> She scaled the Indian meal with the salted boiling water, made it into a dough, rolled it thinly and cut it into little scones. A bed was made on the hearth by raking amongst the ashes on all sides. Each scone was rolled in a cabbage leaf and placed on a bed with hot ashes piled on top and left until cooked. The scorched leaf was then turned back to disclose fragrant little cakes which were delicious with rasher gravy and egg yolk (Laverty 2004: 86).

Anyone who has ever made proper Mexican corn tortillas will realise the similarity in the method of pouring boiling water over the corn masa and making it into a dough.

Growing up in North-west Donegal, Annette Sweeney remembers her mother baking Indian meal scone (in Donegal, a 'scone of bread' was a circular-shaped bread dough with a criss-cross on top, baked flat on a tray in the oven, like the traditional brown scone/bread): 'While my mother regularly made a brown scone and occasionally a treacle scone, it is her "Indian meal" scone that really stands out as a food memory. I loved its colour, gritty texture and aroma and it was baked a few times a week. Served with butter and homemade jam, it was delicious.'

Cornmeal is hard to come by these days, so if you're going to make this bread at home, you can use polenta instead, which is widely available.

O I O
Breakfast roll

Many a house was built on breakfast rolls. As building work boomed during the Celtic Tiger, queues of construction workers would wait in line for their breakfast roll. They became so famous, the comedian Pat Shortt even wrote a song, 'Jumbo Breakfast Roll', about them that was a No. 1 hit for six weeks.

A breakfast roll usually consists of a white baguette filled with sausages, bacon, black and white pudding, butter, mushrooms, tomatoes and tomato ketchup or brown sauce. It's more of a meal than a breakfast. A regular breakfast roll contains a whopping 1,200 calories.

They are now part of our food heritage in Ireland, if only of the last 25 years. It is even said that the breakfast roll was our 'national dish' of the Celtic Tiger period (B. McDonald 2008). They even found their way into the Irish language: *rollóg bhricfeasta*.

Their place in the Irish food story is now secured by the enduring image of the Breakfast Roll Man, a mythical figure from the 1990s and 2000s, most often a builder, who devoured them daily.

Though the era of the breakfast roll in Ireland has now passed, faded into history like a spurious Greek myth, it can still be found occasionally, most likely alongside its replacement: the breakfast burrito.

These vicissitudes demonstrate the often-entertaining aspects of the Irish food story and the ways in which we can never know which way it may turn next.

O I I

Burgers

I'd love to tell you that my first burger was from an old-school chipper, many of which were set up by Italian families over the course of the 20th century, with names like Sorrento's and Mario's, but it wasn't. Trips to McDonald's on the Long Mile Road were a highlight of my youth. Granted, they were only on special occasions, such as communions, birthdays and confirmations. When my parents made burgers at home, they were never as sexy as those McDonald's ones. Or so I thought at the time. I question those memories now, but nostalgia, especially food nostalgia, pushes back against past reality.

Even my grandparents went to McDonald's. They would have never dreamed of making hamburgers for dinner at home, though we often ate a meat patty (a burger without the bun) for lunch (which was dinner), served around 12:30. We ate it with a knife and fork. To this day, I often eat food made for eating without cutlery, such as burgers and pizzas, with a knife and fork. I love to cut a burger into quarters with a knife, and only then pick it up. A strange practice, I admit, but one that surely is a hangover from the Victorian sensibility of not eating with your hands.

You can't talk about chippers without talking about two burgers: the battered burger and the spice burger. The battered burger is pretty much what it says on the tin: a burger dipped in batter and deep-fried. Delicious after a few pints; not so delicious without any. Such is the allure of Irish food after dark.

The spice burger was invented by Maurice Walsh in his own butcher shop in Glasnevin in Dublin in the early 1950s. Walsh Family Foods went on to sell the product all over Ireland and it ended up on many chipper menus. Made with only 20% meat, I wonder what else was in it, but Irish people loved it. It's now available to buy in plenty of supermarkets in the frozen section.

012

Butter

The first time I made butter, I was 33 years old. I thought I was witnessing a miracle. I watched the cream, which we had fermented overnight, split and then gradually turn into two substances: butter and buttermilk. I suddenly realised why it was called buttermilk: it was the milk from the butter! You might think that the story of a chef who had never made butter or didn't know why buttermilk was called buttermilk is a funny story or a sad one, but you'd be surprised how many people have never made butter in their life. It's just something that we don't have to do anymore. We produce vast quantities of butter in Ireland and export over 90% of it around the world. Alongside beef, dairy is our biggest industry.

Once upon a time, there were many butters in Ireland. The Cork Butter Exchange was world-famous. As late as the 1970s, many small butter-makers were still dotted around the country. Photos from the Irish Butter Museum in Cork are testament to this diversity. While there are still a few small butter-makers in Ireland, nearly everyone knows the name of Kerrygold, which is set to become the first trillion-dollar Irish company in the world.

Historically, butter was as good as money in Ireland. Rent and tributes could be paid in butter. Butter was so valuable, it was often buried to keep it safe. Butter that has been found stashed in peat bogs may have been a result of this, although scholars speculate whether the butter was perhaps a ritual offering to the gods rather than a foodstuff being stored in the bog to preserve it. We now refer to this kind of butter as bog butter. The oldest bog butter found to date in Ireland is from the 1st century AD.

OI3

Cabbage

Though wild forms of brassicas have existed in Ireland long before people, the cultivated kind did not arrive here until the 16th century. Bacon and cabbage is the one everyone knows best, but other cabbage dishes abound in Ireland, such as creamed cabbage, cabbage with drawn butter, Scotch cabbage (because of the seeds coming from Scotland), cabbage salad and, of course, colcannon.

Along with the potato, cabbage was the most important vegetable for the native Irish for many centuries (Hickey 2018). Cabbage soup is mentioned in the 12th-century Irish poem *The Vision of MacConglinne*, which tells the story of a 'hungry scholar from Armagh' who visits the greatest 'gourmandizer in Ireland, King Cathal Mac Finguine of Munster' (Mahon 1991: 5). For those doubting food production and consumption in Ireland during this time, a read of this poem lays bare the rich food culture present in Ireland in the Middle Ages.

When he was travelling around Ireland in the 18th century, Arthur Young (1887) mentions both Scotch cabbages and 'sour crout'. Red cabbage was often served (and still is) with game, such as venison, pigeon and wild duck. The red cabbage would be sliced and cooked with spices, honey and dried fruit, such as sultanas.

For many 20th-century visitors to Ireland, such as the British food writer Jane Grigson, it appeared that cabbage was an unfortunate icon of Irish food:

> To know that cabbages were once the only vegetables people had in some parts of Europe does not mean much. To experience it is another manner. We spent a fortnight in northern Donegal in the summer of 1950. We left with the impression that all the Irish ever ate was cabbage, potatoes, poor quality lamb and Victoria sponge. No wonder they took to whiskey. The village smelled intensely of cabbage every day at noon (cited in Hickey 2018: 212–13).

014
Candy & confectionery

Boiled sweets

After school, we would run to Barton's to get boiled sweets. They were all lined up in jars behind the counter, so old Miss Barton had to take down each jar to weigh out want you wanted, only to put it back on the shelf again. This cycle would be repeated until you had got all your sweets in a little brown bag. Occasionally some of the kids would distract Miss Barton while others crammed their pockets with any chocolates they could get their hands on.

An evening ritual at my grandma's in Mount Merrion in Dublin was sucking Fox's mints while watching evening telly. If a movie was on, you might get a few more than usual if you were good. It seems all Irish households had boxes of boiled sweets lying around. Perhaps it was because so many of that generation abstained from alcohol. If you couldn't have a glass, you'd more than likely suck a sweet.

Rock

They may as well have been rocks and they destroyed your teeth, but rock was something you always seemed to eat on your holidays, especially by the sea. Perhaps the warmer weather was supposed to soften the sugar before you broke your teeth on it.

Though they normally came in the shape of sticks, you would occasionally find one in the shape of a dummy (a child's soother). The interesting thing about rock sticks is there was often something written inside them, and no matter where you broke the stick, the writing was the same. On visits to Knock you could get Knock rock, which was the colour of the Irish flag and had the word *Knock* written inside.

Toffee

Though Welsh in origin, toffee quickly spread to Ireland (via England and Scotland) and was enjoyed by many Irish people. Toffee can be either hard or soft. There were always a few bags lying around my grandma's sitting room. Like mints, I suppose they were something to suck while watching evening television. Some varieties have a soft liquid butterscotch centre, while others are more fudge-like. Yellowman, or yallaman, is an Irish-style toffee that was often sold at markets, particularly in the North of the country. We serve a rose fudge in Aniar as part of our petit four in honour of this Irish toffee tradition.

Wham Bars

Wham Bars, Roy of the Rover, Stinger, Drumstick, Toxic Waste – they were all sweet, sticky bars that would pull the teeth out of your head. We ate them all.

These bars had sour sugar crystals and sherbet embedded in them that would make your mouth water as you chewed. The fizz from the sour aspects of the bar gave the eater an unforgettable experience. Many of these bars are no longer manufactured, but Wham Bars are still around. At the height of their production, over 30 million bars a year were made.

John Millar (1826–96), of Millar's Confectionery Company (which eventually merged with McCowan's, who made Wham Bars), observed that 'sweets are first tasted with the eye, but flavour is the heart and soul of all confectionery' (Millar McCowan). He knew what us kids wanted: coloured chewy sugar with a sour kick.

015
Carageen moss pudding

Many cultures have some type of cream pudding. For example, panna cotta is an Italian dessert of 'cooked' cream with sugar, gelatine and various flavours, such as vanilla, fruit or coffee. Traditionally, panna cotta is made with one part cream and one part milk, though I use buttermilk to give it an Irish twist. The Irish version of a cream pudding is made with carrageen moss, a type of seaweed.

Though Myrtle Allen made carrageen moss pudding famous in her restaurant in Ballymaloe House (it still has a place on the dessert trolley there), it existed long before her. A recipe from Donegal is included in Florence Irwin's *The Cookin' Woman: Irish Country Recipes* (1949).

Seaweed is not for everyone, which explains the popularity of gelatine for making a traditional set cream. Carageen moss pudding is a variation of the classic blancmange, which is made with gelatine instead of carrageen. Most recipes use sugar, but I prefer to sweeten the pudding with honey. However, there are powdered seaweed alternatives such as kappa that are derived from carrageen.

Set cream and milk puddings were popular in Ireland from at least the 18th century. In my research for *The Irish Cookbook* (McMahon 2020), I came across a recipe for a 'burnt cream' in the recipe book of Mrs Dot Drew of Mocollop Castle near Ballyduff in Co. Waterford that appeared in Darina Allen's *Irish Traditional Cooking* (1995). Interestingly, the recipe was similar to the Spanish crema catalana that we serve in our restaurant Cava, which demonstrates – as much of the food in this book does – the way in which food travels unimpeded through different cultures.

To some degree, Irish food is a tale of two halves: the inexpensive, processed commodity on the one hand and artisan food with a sense of place on the other. It was almost as if after independence, we couldn't decide who or what we wanted to be.

016

Cheese

To some degree, Irish food is a tale of two halves: the inexpensive, processed commodity on the one hand and artisan food with a sense of place on the other. It was almost as if after independence, we couldn't decide who or what we wanted to be. Or was it that we didn't want to become an island of posh cheese like the French? Their cheese had notions; ours was basic.

While there may be a little truth in this – Éamon de Valera's comely maidens eating Calvita cheese while dancing at the crossroads – the reality is much more complex, from independence and cultural wars to post-war hardships, stagnation and isolation. To this day, we still push and pull against our farmhouse cheeses, often afraid to support them in case we get accused of being elitist in terms of our food.

The women who revived the Irish farmhouse cheese movement in the late 1960s and early 1970s looked abroad; they looked back to look forward. The likes of Milleens, Gubbeen, Durrus and Cashel Blue all emerged from this period.

This is not to forget the long history of cheese production in Ireland. Curd (the most basic form of cheese) was a popular food in Ireland from pre-Christian times up until the 18th century (Mahon 1991: 91). The 12th-century text *The Vision of MacConglinne* speaks of cheese-making and the making of curds. As well as a foodstuff, curds were used to cure many ailments in Gaelic Ireland.

Whey, the by-product of making cheese, was also used, mainly as a protein-rich drink for monks in medieval monasteries. In the late 1600s, the English bookseller and writer John Dunton (2003) described cheese-making practices among peasants in Connemara. Unfortunately, these cheeses do not seem to have acquired the same reputation that their French, Spanish and Italian counterparts did. We had to wait for the Irish farmhouse cheese revival to take our place among the great cheese-makers of the world.

0 1 7

Chicken

It's hard to think of a time when people in Ireland didn't eat chicken nearly every day, but before World War Two, rabbit was much more common and chickens (or rather, hens) were kept for their eggs. When the hens had laid all they could, then, and only then, would they go into the pot. Braising older birds makes them more tender. A roast chicken was a Sunday treat for many households and would have been reserved for special occasions.

Due to our penchant for bacon and ham, many Irish recipes for chicken include these foodstuffs, often in the form of chicken wrapped in bacon or chicken and ham pies, casseroles or hotpots. The traditional dish of a whole chicken cooked with cider, bacon and white cabbage is one such dish that demonstrates this in the Irish food story. Dumplings were common in chicken stews, as were apples or other autumn fruit when in season. Later in the 20th century, American influence began to be felt in the form of chicken Maryland appearing on menus around the country.

Chicken à la king

I somehow imagined that chicken à la king was a distinctly Irish dish, as it was the most-requested 'wet' dish when we used to do outdoor catering. Yet no one had any idea where this dish came from.

In the early days of the internet, it was harder to find information about obscure bits of food history, let alone how a dish related to Ireland. I remember coming across it in *Larousse Gastronomique* around 2002. It classed *poulet à la reine* as a 'term applied to a number of elegant and delicate dishes from classic French cuisine', sometimes made with sweetbreads and truffles. I was dubious about this dish's relationship to the Irish chicken à la king, which certainly didn't include sweetbread or truffles.

Ironically, all the origin stories of the dish (bar one) come from 19th-century England. The only American story associates the dish with its supposed inventor, William 'Bill' King, in and around 1890. His obituary in the *New-York Tribune* (1915) stated:

> The name of William King is not listed among the great ones of the earth. No monuments will ever be erected to his memory, for he was only a cook. Yet what a cook! In him blazed the fire of genius which, at the white heat of inspiration, drove him one day, in the old Bellevue, in Philadelphia, to combine bits of chicken, mushrooms, truffles, red and green peppers and cream in that delight-some mixture which ever after has been known as Chicken à la King.

The recipe was also mentioned in the *New York Times* in 1893 and was eventually published in *The Fannie Farmer Cookbook* in 1906.

Still, how did it get to Galway and become one of the most popular chicken dishes there? Was it due to its popularity in America during the 20th century? Did it somehow make it back over to Ireland as a vol-au-vent filling? Vol-au-vents (a historical French dish from around 1739 that travelled to Mexico and Pakistan) were extremely popular in Ireland in the 1970s. They have made a bit of a comeback in recent years, with recipes from Irish chefs such as Kevin Dundon and Brian McDermott, both with chicken fillings that could be described as chicken à la king.

Chicken fillet roll

The chicken fillet roll is probably the most popular sandwich in Ireland nowadays and is currently being touted as 'Irish street food' in London. It's essentially a breaded chicken fillet in a Cuisine de France bread roll with a selection of other 'salad' toppings. You can get one at every petrol station and deli counter in the country. Many of the 'fillets' for chicken fillet rolls come from what is called the 'third breast' of the chicken. Put simply, all the meat and scraps are hoovered off a chicken carcass and reformed into a 'breast' with the addition of loads of other stuff. Is mechanically reformed meat a no-waste solution? I'm not sure. I think ultimately it's about profit and price.

A poll in 2020 listed the chicken fillet roll as 'Ireland's favourite deli food' (Brent 2020), so it won't be leaving the annals of the Irish food story anytime soon.

o I 8

Chips

'A proper bag of chips, laced in salt and vinegar, with a portion of curry' – so say Eugene and Ronan Greaney, aka the Dough Bros, when asked about iconic Irish foods. Especially, they add, 'after a few pinteens.' The Irish do love a curry cheese chip.

Chips at home invariably meant frozen ready-made chips, although some households did make their own. Una Ní Bhroin recalls her mam making homemade chips and serving them 'with fish floured and fried on the pan, and peas from a tin and raw carrots'. I can't remember when the deep-fryer came into our house, but I do recall chips and all sorts of other things being cooked in it. My nana never bought one; she just heated oil in a pot on her gas cooker, cooking with a half-smoked cigarette in her mouth and a bandana wrapped around her head to protect her hair. I don't think she ever realised the dangers. Many Irish people still have a fear of deep-fryers precisely because of the many home fires that were caused by cooking chips this way.

As for the cooking fat for frying chips, we were a Crisp 'n Dry household (wasn't everyone?), which meant everything was fried in sunflower oil. Proper chippers used lard, huge blocks of it. When we ran our own gastropub, we would fry the chips in duck fat. Though your heart may not thank you, your taste-buds certainly will.

Chip sandwich/butty

Carbs on carbs with some fat – that's how I would describe a chip sandwich. But when you want to let everything go, there is nothing better. It's also a cost-effective meal. Nice thick chips from the local chipper, bread and loads of butter. Maybe a little tomato ketchup or brown sauce for additional flavour and acidity. Whatever the bread and whether or not you add cheese, ketchup or brown sauce, the chip sandwich (or the chip butty from the chipper) is an iconic Irish sandwich that still stands the test of time.

019
Christmas cake/pudding

Each year, my grandma made a dozen or so Christmas cakes. My father tells me she wasn't much of a baker, though she baked her own brown bread. But Christmas cake was different. It's still a tradition in many houses around the country.

Time is an often-overlooked factor in baking and cooking. The wait for the Christmas cake or pudding to mature is something that words fail to describe, like the way we wait for certain drinks, such as wine and whiskey, to achieve their potential.

In the days of open fires, the Christmas pudding mixture was formed into a ball, wrapped in cloth and set 'to boil in a big pot on the fire on Christmas Eve night' for at least 'ten hours' (Mahon 1991). An older version, called cutlin, was made of a spiced porridge of wheaten meal mixed with 'sugar, dried fruits, and spices' (Mahon 1991: 145). For my money, nothing beats Monica Sheridan's recipe from *The Art of Irish Cooking* (1965). Sheridan was Ireland's first celebrity chef. Her recipe was first published in the *Irish Times* in 1955 and was subsequently made the world over, from Rome and Hong Kong to Trinidad (Sheridan 1965: 139).

In Clare Keegan's short novel *Small Things Like These* (2021), which is set during Christmas in Ireland in 1985, the character Eileen Furlong makes a Christmas cake according to an Odlums recipe. This recipe, which was included on the back of a bag of Odlums flour at Christmastime, was a staple for many households during that decade (at the time of writing, it's available on the Odlums website). As the character Eileen remarks, 'Is there anything lovelier than a slice of Christmas cake with tea after a walk on Christmas Day?'

020

Cider

Drinking cider was, and perhaps still is, a rite of passage in Ireland. You got your Junior Cert results, then you went and drank a load of cider: Bulmers, Scrumpy Jack, White Lightning and Linden Village. At my first open-air concert at Slane, Co. Meath in 1995 (I was there to see REM and Oasis), I encountered a young man with a large plastic bottle of cider. I asked him where he had got it. 'Linden Village', he replied, so off I went up the road, walking away from Slane Castle in search of Linden Village (for those who don't know, as I obviously didn't at the time, Linden Village is a brand of cider, not a place in Meath).

The earliest mention of cider in an Irish text is in a 12th-century document from Ulster. During the monastic age in Ireland, monks made cider.

The term for cider in the Irish language is *leann úll*, which means 'apple beer'. Apples have been eaten in Ireland for thousands of years, so we can assume that cider or some type of apple beer was also produced during that time.

We have a rich tradition of cider-making in Ireland, though for most of modern history the drink was almost forgotten. Cider production in Ireland was a major industry from the 16th century onwards due to the immigration of Huguenots from France and Palatines from Germany, who brought cider-making skills with them when they fled their respective countries due to persecution.

The counties most associated with apple production in the past were Armagh, Kilkenny, Tipperary and Waterford. The English travel writer Richard Pococke toured Ireland in 1752, noting that Affane, Co. Waterford was famous for its cider and that Shannongrove near Pallaskenry in Co. Limerick had a cider house (Pococke 1891).

Cider-making went into decline during the Famine (1845–49). Despite government efforts, which produced a short revival in the

Drinking cider was, and perhaps still is, a rite of passage in Ireland.

late 19th century, the industry was hit hard again by the War of Independence, the Irish Civil War and the two world wars.

In 1935, Willian Magner began commercial cider production in Clonmel, South Tipperary. In 1937, English cider-maker H.P. Bulmer purchased a 50% share in the business. In 1946, Bulmers purchased the remaining 50% and changed the name of the company to Bulmers Ltd Clonmel. Bulmers is still a popular cider in Ireland and is sold under the name Magners outside of Ireland.

A viable craft cider industry only returned to Ireland in the 21st century. This is promising, though that is not to say it will regain a place in the Irish drinks pantheon. There are still only about 20 craft cider producers in Ireland. It wasn't until 2000 that David Llewellyn began producing craft cider for the Irish market and began a quiet, slow revolution. Highbank Orchards is another great cider producer who also make a variety of drinks on their 17th-century organic orchard in Kilkenny. Lastly, Cockagee cider, produced in Meath by Mark Jenkinson, is a naturally sparkling keeved cider. Keeving is an ancient technique whereby the fresh-pressed cloudy apple juice is clarified by a natural pectin gel that traps any particles and impurities.

Writing in *Sláinte: The Complete Guide to Irish Craft Beer and Cider*, Hennessy and Jensen (2014: 74) state that 'cider made from Cockagee apples could even pass for wine.' They go on to say:

> In fact, some of the best ciders have even been compared to champagne [...] Emma Tyrrell of Cider Ireland says, 'We are seeing people serve a dry cider instead of champagne at wedding receptions. Maybe it's the "Buy Irish" thing, but served in a flute with canapés like black pudding bites and devils on horseback, it seems to go down a treat.'

Cider should be our national wine, so let's hope that someday the Irish craft cider industry has its day in the sun and features on more restaurant drinks menus and as part of a drinks pairing for tasting menus. Our Irish drinks pairing at Aniar features Irish wine, Irish cider and Irish beer. However, as with the cheese produced in Ireland, the debate will always swing between craft and commercial when it comes to producing cider.

Cidona

Cidona is a popular Irish sparkling apple-based drink that is produced by using fermented apple juice. Thus, the drink retains the flavour of cider without the alcohol. An English version was sold from the 1940s as an alternative to drinking alcohol. In 1940, it was advertised on UK radio by Bulmers as 'the newest, non-alcoholic, sparkling apple drink' and priced at 10 pence for a 'big 5 glass flagon'.

In Ireland, Cidona was originally made by Bulmers in Tipperary from 1955 until it was sold to Britvic in 2007. Due to the popularity of cider in pubs, Cidona was always on offer for those who weren't drinking or for all the children who would inevitably be running around the pub.

O 2 I

Coddle

Coddle – or Dublin coddle, to be more precise – is a dish made of leftover sausages and bacon. Traditionally, the sausages and bacon were cut up and combined with onions and potatoes and left to stew in a light broth. Though often unappetising to look at ('boiled mickeys' was how one woman described coddle to me), the dish was made famous by several Irish writers, including Jonathan Swift, James Joyce and Seán O'Casey.

Essentially, it's a dish that grew out of poverty and famine, then migrated into the working-class areas of Dublin at the beginning of the 20th century to become a dish of central importance to the people who lived there. It often contained a drop of Guinness or it was eaten with plenty of pints and soda bread. It's said that housewives would prepare the coddle during the day and it would sit on the stove until the men returned home from the pub. The word itself is derived from the verb 'to coddle' or 'to cook' (from the French *caulder*).

Given its associations with poverty, it's surprising to find 'authentic' recipes, especially because the dish was traditionally made with whatever leftovers were to hand (as in pig's trotters, pork ribs, etc.). Some associate it with the Catholic Church's insistence on abstaining from meat on a Friday – coddle was a way of using up the bacon and sausages on a Thursday. It was often served at funerals in the past; Jonathan Swift, who enjoyed the dish, remarked as much.

Many contemporary chefs are revisiting coddle and putting their own spin on it, from adding barley to using ham hocks instead of bacon. I always fry the sausages first to give them a little colour, but this practice is not allowed when making a traditional coddle. Nothing incites more outrage or controversy in Ireland than browning the sausages in coddle.

022

Coffee

Coffee and Ireland have a longer history than many think, even though we were later to the party than most of Europe. As a colony of the British Empire, we had access to products from all over the world. Indeed, there was probably more international produce in Ireland before independence than there was afterwards. When we got rid of British rule in Ireland, we also got rid of an international dimension to food for at least 50 years. A narrative of self-sufficiency, coupled with a trade war, had big impacts on the Irish food story.

Coffee first arrived in Ireland in the 17th century via Venetian traders who brought the beans back from their travels to the Middle East and North Africa. In the Inchiquin Papers in the National Library, which date from 1663, a 'coffee pott and plate' are included in the inventory of the house. At first it was the aristocratic classes that enjoyed it, namely the Anglo-Irish Big House landowners who adopted British and European tastes from the 17th century to the early 20th century.

Coffee shops began opening all around Ireland during the 18th century, starting in Dublin, Cork, Limerick, Kilkenny and Wexford, then Galway and later in Belfast and Waterford. The most famous coffee house of the 20th century in Ireland was Bewley's on Grafton Street. Though it opened in 1927 (complete with Harry Clarke stained-glass windows), the original café goes back to the 19th century.

In 1835, Samuel Bewley and his son Charles brought 2,000 chests of tea directly from China to Dublin. Five years later, another family member, Joshua Bewley, embarked on an innovative and revolutionary business journey, establishing a tea shop called the China Tea Company.

The first Bewley's café opened on George's Street in Dublin in 1894. The café sold tea and was the first to roast coffee in-store. Interestingly, Ernest Bewley (Joshua's son) imported the first Jersey cows into

Ireland from Jersey Island in 1903 to supply the growing demand for good-quality milk and cream for his cafés and bakery in Dublin.

As well as Bewley's, there were two other notable coffee companies in Ireland: Findlater and Robert Roberts. In 1823, Alexander Findlater set up his business on Burgh Quay opposite the Custom House importing coffee, tea and wine into Ireland. Findlater & Co. is still in existence today, more than 200 years later.

Robert Roberts, which merged with Findlater in 2017, has been roasting and blending coffee in Dublin since 1905. Robert Roberts had coffee houses in Suffolk Street and later on Grafton Street. It was here that Lady Gregory convened her PEN literary society and Maud Gonne McBride was a regular customer.

Though tea dominated Irish drink culture for most of the 20th century, the arrival of American coffeeshops such as Starbucks turned coffee into the dominant drink in the capital from the 1990s onwards. An article in the *Irish Times* in 2021 even declared Dublin the second-most 'coffee-obsessed' capital city in the world (Dennison 2021). Our love of coffee is part of a tradition in Ireland that goes back 400 years. However, we still drink marginally more tea in the country as a whole – 45% of the population drinks tea daily compared to 42% who drink coffee (Buckley et al. 2021).

As well as loving coffee, the Irish (or at least people visiting Ireland) also love whiskey, hence the widespread availably of Irish coffees.

○ 2 3

Corn

Corn seemed to feature in my childhood in one way or another, whether it was in the ubiquitous combination of tuna and sweetcorn or the tinned sweetcorn my mother put in the shepherd's pie (I recall my youngest brother, Alex, taking a particular dislike to sweetcorn, so much so that he would pick it out of the shepherd's pie one kernel at a time). Its use on those do-it-yourself Superquinn pizzas was the apogee of my early years.

Though corn is a grain and a type of maize, sweetcorn is picked when young, called the milk stage, and used as a vegetable. Sweetcorn stores poorly and must be eaten fresh, canned or frozen, before the kernels become tough and starchy, which is why it appears on the cob in supermarkets for only brief periods of time when it's in season.

Corn (in the form of maize) was an important foodstuff during the Famine years in Ireland. The cornmeal arrived by boat from the Americas imported by the British government, led by Prime Minster Robert Peel, due to the failure of the potato crop. Kate Ryan (2022) writes:

> As a Famine relief food, corn should have been an ideal intervention, packed with protein and niacin. But knowledge of grinding and nixtamalization, the keys to unlocking those nutrients, did not travel with the corn. Ireland lacked the technology to grind corn fine enough, and without lime for nixtamalization, the importance of steeping corn for long periods and double cooking was unknown. Without these two processes, many people suffered from pellagra – a disease associated with improperly prepared corn – leading to skin irritation, diarrhoea, mouth ulcers, sickness and worse. This second misery visited among the starving Irish earned corn the moniker 'Peel's brimstone'.

However, it eventually found its way into many different dishes, such as yellow bread, porridge and dumplings (Sexton 1998: 91).

0 2 4

Crisps

The fact that we love crisps so much often confirms the stereotype of Ireland's relationship to potatoes. There are almost as many crisps as there are weeks in the year.

While a New York chef named George Crum is credited with inventing crisps in Cary Moon's Lake Lodge (or Lake House) restaurant in Saratoga Springs, New York, in 1853, they existed in both England and Ireland before this date. The earliest recipe for crisps seems to be William Kitchiner's 'potato chips' in his best-selling book on both sides of the Atlantic, *The Cook's Oracle* (1822). But perhaps it was the popularity of Crum's creation that bequeathed us the modern crisp, even though potato chips (crisps to us) were not mass-produced until the 20th century. There is even a brand called Saratoga Chips that is still operating today.

In England, Frank Smith sold salted crisps in greaseproof paper bags to pubs in London from 1913 onwards. However, it was the Irish who brought the most flavour to the potato crisp. In 1954, Joe 'Spud' Murphy, the owner of the Irish crisps company Tayto, produced the world's first seasoned crisps: cheese and onion. In England, Frank Smith responded with a salt and vinegar flavour. The crisp wars had begun.

To further complicate things, Tayto sold the naming rights and recipe to the Hutchinson family in Northen Ireland in 1956, which is why we have two different Tayto crisps on the island of Ireland.

While Tayto crisps are the king of all crisps in Ireland, there are many other crisp varieties here, probably as many as there are ice creams. While the battle between Tayto and King may be well and truly over (isn't it?), other crisps, such as Pringles (which are not technically a crisp, as they don't have enough potato in them), seem to attract the young people of today. There are also some great artisan brands emerging to challenge the market. While I am partial to a variety of other crisps, such as Burger Bites, KP Skips Prawn Cocktail,

Chickatees, Chipsticks, Hunky Dory and Monster Munch (the Tayto brand is called Mighty Munch), Tayto cheese and onion will always be my No. 1 Irish crisp.

Though the crisp is now an international food, we would do well to remember the Irish contribution to it. However, a distinct Irish flavour is still wanting. In Belgium, Bolognese-flavoured potato crisps are popular, while in Japan you can get both chilli scallop-flavoured and salmon teriyaki-flavoured crisps. Could an oyster-flavoured crisp be the answer to our problem?

Crisp sandwich

When I asked my editor if I could include a recipe for a crisp sandwich in *The Irish Cookbook* (McMahon 2020), she smiled wryly. A moment later, she replied, 'Why not?' And so it was that the crisp sandwich took its place in the pantheon of Irish foods that make us what we are today.

Aer Lingus, the Irish national airline, tapped into the crisp sandwich market for a while with their 'make it yourself' crisp sandwich that they served on short-haul and European flights between 2015 and 2016. The 'mile-high' snack included a packet of Tayto crisps, a small pat of Kerrygold butter, two slices of bread and a little plastic knife (Ó Conghaile 2015). Much to the dismay of their customers, and despite great sales, Aer Lingus discontinued the sandwich.

The important things about crisp sandwiches are that they are made with regular sliced pan, lashings of good butter and Tayto cheese and onion crisps. Of course, there are those who argue that other crisps, such as King crisps, can be used instead. Growing up, I remember sticking all sorts of crisps, such as Hula Hoops and Monster Munch, into a sandwich. Though most people favour the cheese and onion flavour in their crisp sandwich, the world is your oyster when it comes to making a crisp sandwich.

025

Cucumbers

Though cucumbers originated in India, they have been in Britain and Ireland since the 14th century. The popularity of the cucumber sandwich reached its apex in the Edwardian period due to cheap labour and plentiful coal, which allowed cucumbers to be produced in hotbeds under glasshouses year round.

In the first act of Oscar Wilde's play *The Importance of Being Earnest*, cucumber sandwiches that have been ordered and prepared for Lady Bracknell's visit are all eaten beforehand by her nephew Algernon. This not only points to Algernon's duplicity but also to the social standing that these sandwiches held in Britain and in Ireland among the upper echelons of society.

There is more to cucumbers than just sandwiches. Cucumber ketchup was once a thing in Ireland and the UK. Cucumbers and oysters also work well. Theodora FitzGibbon's book *Irish Traditional Food* (1983) includes a cucumber sauce for fish such as salmon. While I'm all in favour of using cucumber in a myriad of ways with fish, the 18th-century penchant in Anglo-Irish Big Houses for stuffing and braising them with minced meat is perhaps best forgotten. My favourite way to use cucumbers in Aniar is to char them with a blowtorch and serve them with mackerel, oyster mayonnaise and fresh sea herbs.

026

Cuisine de France

On my return from a failed trip to try to make a living in Paris as a young poet (I was in awe of Samuel Beckett), I took to buying large Cuisine de France baguettes and eating them with a cheap wheel of Brie from the local supermarket. How sophisticated am I, I thought, with my bread, my cheese, my wine and my copy of *Waiting for Godot*.

Brought up on a diet of soda bread, sliced pan and the odd soft roll filled with ham and egg mayonnaise, I think we were all enamoured of Cuisine de France bread and croissants when they arrived in the shops in 1989, 'baked in store daily'. They forgot to add that they were baked in store daily from frozen, but we didn't care. We loved these French baguettes.

We did care, however, that the bread would turn too quickly. The following day, it was harder than a lump hammer. When we were kids, we would often use them as swords when they were past their best – the longer baguette was great for hitting my brother over the head. We were used to eating soda bread on its third day, still as fresh as the day it was made (or perhaps we just imagined it was because we put so much butter on it).

But during the wonder of those first years of Cuisine de France in Ireland, we all felt a little more European. It was as if someone had built an invisible bridge made of bread that connected us directly to Paris.

027

Curry

While writing *The Irish Cookbook* (McMahon 2020) I came across a recipe for lobster curry in the National Library. It was from Mayo of all places. Who would have thought they had curry there in the early 19th century? Potato curry goes back even further and can be found in the 18th century in Ireland. After serving in the English Raj army in India, many Irish soldiers returned with packets of curry powder to spice up their spuds. Like our British neighbours, we have always been partial to a curry.

While curry might not go back as far as Cuchulain, it has been in Ireland since before the French Revolution. Curry powder was first exported to Britain in the 18th century by the British East India Company. The word *curry* is an anglicised word derived from *kari*, which means a sauce made from the leaves of the tree. Ireland and India have many things in common, not least our history of colonisation.

Curry also pops up in Florence Irwin's cookbook, *The Cookin' Woman* (1949), in mulligatawny soup. Curried eggs would also have been popular in Ireland, though perhaps only for the more 'adventurous households' (Hickey 2018: 137).

My first taste of curry was McDonnells Original Curry Powder. Anyone who has ever had curry chips, curry cheese chips or a 3-in-1 (chips, curry and rice: a classic Irish invention) will know the flavour of this potent curry powder. Just add water and wham! A full-on curry flavour. It's still available in Irish supermarkets and chippers around the country. In fact, curry is now one of the top 10 dishes made at home by Irish people (Pope 2020).

028

Custard cream slice

Custard cream slices have been a feature of Irish bakeries since at least the 1950s. As with many pastries, we have made the custard cream slice our own.

The custard cream slice is actually a *mille-feuille*, whose modern form goes back to Marie-Antoine Carême, a French pastry chef from the 19th century. It most likely entered Ireland via the traditional *mille-feuille*, which is made of three layers of puff pastry and two layers of crème pâtissière, whereas the Irish one has only two layers of puff pastry and just one layer of pastry cream in the middle. The top of the Irish custard cream slice is always glazed with icing and feathered with dark chocolate. It is this feathered feature that I remember from my childhood, peering through the curved glass of the pastry display case of the Elite Bakery and Confectionery in Maynooth all those years ago.

For Irish pastry chef Aoife Noonan (2021):

> Custard slices remind me of nostalgic Sunday treats, with a quick stop in the local bakery on the way home from visiting grandparents. Glass shelves lined with buns and pastries, plump and golden, stuffed with cream and jam. Dad always chose the cream bun, and mum the coffee slice. It was the vanilla custard slice that sealed the deal for me. I couldn't resist the crisp, sweet puff pastry and that thick, canary-yellow custard. The nice lady in the hairnet packaged them up for us and said she'd see us again next week. It was our Sunday ritual.

029
Dingle pie

Not many Irish foods are associated with a particular town. Of course, we have many that are related to different regions, such as Connemara Mountain lamb or Lough Neagh smoked eel, but foods from specific towns or cities are less common.

Dingle pie, also called mutton pie, is probably the most famous pie in Ireland. In terms of its lineage, it's related to the pies of Northern England and to Cornish pasties.

As well as being sold in Dingle and Listowel in Co. Kerry, they were sold every August at the Puck Fair in Killorglin. The main business of the Puck Fair is buying and selling livestock. A puck is a large goat, which was hoisted high up over the crowds in celebration. According to legend, this was to commemorate the 'noise of the herd of goats led by the puck' warning the native Irish of approaching English soldiers (FitzGibbon 1983: 119). However, it may also be a fair associated with a 'pre-Christian deity' (FitzGibbon 1983: 120).

The pies would be sold warm and dipped in beef gravy. The pastry was originally made with lamb fat, but nowadays butter is more common. Moreover, the meat would generally have been mutton due to the value placed on lamb. Given the resurgence of pies in recent years, let's hope that Dingle pies begin appearing on menus around the country.

030

Donegal Catch

In my early teens, I went through a year or two of eating only this frozen battered fish. It was my way of trying to get some fish into me. The ads on the telly were cool and I thought why not? There weren't any bones in this frozen, breaded fish, so I wasn't going to choke if I ate it. Fish meant fear, but not Donegal Catch. No one ever died eating Donegal Catch.

Donegal Catch has been around since 1984 and is still going strong. Its television advertisements are legendary, particularly the commercials 'Filing Cabinet' (2015) and 'Taken' (2020). Ironically, its processing plant is in Sligo. I guess Sligo Catch just doesn't have the same ring to it. Whatever you think of frozen, breaded fish (we all grew up on fish fingers; see page 60), this brand was a stepping stone for a whole generation of Irish people to go out and find a fishmonger to talk to. It wouldn't be until my early twenties that I fell in love with actual fish while travelling in Spain.

Who knows – if it wasn't for Donegal Catch and Captain Bird's Eye fish fingers, many of us may have never eaten fish at all.

O 3 I

Duck

Back in 2015, on Ronan Byrne's farm near Athenry, one of Spain's top chefs, Albert Adrià, was astonished at the quality of Ronan's rotisserie duck cooked over a spit. Adrià was surprised that the world didn't know more about our ducks. We have many world-class duck farmers. Names like Silverhill, Skeaghanore, Thornhill and Regan should be as well-known as our famous sports stars.

Cooking duck, whether it's pan-frying a breast, confiting a leg or roasting one whole, is no more difficult than cooking a chicken. It's a pity more Irish people don't embrace this bird, which has been here for centuries, particularly in farmyards of old. In France they make a dish called *parmentier de confit de canard*, which roughly translates as 'duck cottage pie' or 'duck shepherd's pie.' There's no reason we couldn't make a similar dish in Ireland with our fantastic ducks and potatoes.

Traditionally in Ireland, a duck was braised or roasted whole. If roasted, it would have been stuffed with sage and onions and served with an apple sauce. Often the duck itself was stuffed with apples (with 'a little sugar and a pinch of sage') if they were plentiful (FitzGibbon 1983: 92).

For Margaret Hickey, eating ducks in Ireland was associated with Whitsuntide (a Christian festival of Pentecost that takes place 50 days after Easter). As well as feasting on duck eggs for breakfast, many people in the medieval period in Ireland would have 'boiled their ducks with turnips or parsley and sweet herbs', often adding juniper berries to the pot for additional flavour (Hickey 2018: 144).

032

Eggs

Maynooth in the 1980s was surrounded by farmland; it was practically the countryside. My friend's granny lived beside them and still kept hens. On some Saturday mornings when we didn't go to hurling, my friend and I would go out and gather a few hen's eggs for breakfast. We've largely lost this kind of connection to where food comes from, particularly eggs.

All eggs (chicken, duck and goose) were central to the Irish food experience. In the 12th-century Irish poem *The Vision of MacConglinne*, eggs are referred to as 'pearls of the household.'

Eggs have been an important foodstuff in Ireland for thousands of years. Before the domestication of the chicken, people fed on eggs from wild birds, such as ducks, seagulls, puffins and quails. Large eggs would be boiled or roasted, while small eggs would be sucked out whole from the shell for a nutritious snack on the go. Following the arrival of chickens and other domestic fowl such as geese and ducks, eggs became a central part of the diet in Irish food culture. Chickens were rarely killed; they were kept for their eggs. It seems every new wave of people who came to Ireland, from the Vikings and Normans to the English settlers, brought new ways of cooking eggs to the country.

To preserve eggs in the spring and summer, the eggs would be buttered, that is, covered with butter or lard. Though cold butter was often used, hot butter could also be applied by dipping the egg into a pot of warm melted butter (Sheridan 1965: 94).

When a pot could not be found, eggs would be cooked directly in the ashes of the turf fire, taking around 30 minutes to produce a cooked white with a creamy yolk (Hickey 2018: 138).

Fried eggs, along with fried bread, were a staple in our house and many other houses around the country. Fried eggs could also be had for tea with some rashers (bacon). 'The greatest feast' for her husband, wrote Mary Delany in 1730, was 'fried egg and bacon' (FitzGibbon

1983: 42). We never had poached or baked eggs in our house, but we did have hard-boiled eggs and soldiers (finger-sized pieces of toast) and scrambled eggs.

A wonderful poached egg recipe from the 18th century pairs poached eggs with freshly fried sorrel cooked in butter over a 'slow fire' (FitzGibbon 1983: 43). Interestingly, another recipe from the 19th century includes cayenne pepper, which could not be further from wild sorrel. Other dishes for eggs in Ireland include them being served with fried lettuce (1778) and nettle purée (one by FitzGibbon's grandmother).

In my research in the National Library, I've found some interesting omelette recipes. Perhaps the strangest was an oyster omelette in the Leitrim Papers from the 18th–19th centuries. Though this recipe is from a so-called Big House tradition, it demonstrates the international element in Irish food in the past. Interestingly, a 'Wicklow pancake' is more like an omelette with breadcrumbs and milk as opposed to a traditional Irish pancake.

Irish funerals have a peculiar association with egg sandwiches. Traditionally, these sandwiches would be served with mayonnaise, butter (we love doing both in Ireland) and watercress. At many formal family occasions, trays of triangular egg sandwiches (among others) would float around the living room for all to eat.

In his short novella *Company*, the Irish writer Samuel Beckett tenderly describes his father leaving the house with 'a flask and a package of his favourite egg sandwiches' to avoid 'the pains and general unpleasantness of labour and delivery' of the author (Beckett 1980: 16). Funeral sandwiches at birth, how Beckettian!

033
Findus Crispy Pancakes

When Findus Crispy Pancakes first arrived in our house, I was elated. I thought they were the best thing ever. Popping those frozen pancakes into the oven and watching them turn golden brown through the oven door, I imagined I was in culinary heaven. Could food get any better?

Of course, today I know that food *can* get a lot better, but growing up with repetitive meals of meat, potatoes and vegetables, with fish on Fridays, these pancakes punctuated those dreary, grey dinners. They offered hope for a brighter, more interesting food future.

Findus Crispy Pancakes – a stuffed and breaded pancake that was baked from frozen in the oven – first came on the market in 1958, and by the 1970s they were about as cool as it got in an Irish household. With supermarkets on the rise and freezers being installed in nearly every home, these pancakes (and other ready-made foods) provided respite for the many mothers who had to feed large families.

I'm not the only one in search of a childhood favourite in the form of breadcrumbed pancakes. One of my favourite chefs, Hugh Fearnley-Whittingstall, made his own crispy pancakes stuffed with smoked haddock on his show, *River Cottage*, in November 2009. I'm afraid to make my own now or pop down to the shop and pick some up in case I ruin my memory of them, which is mired in nostalgia. Nostalgia is the name of the game when it comes to certain Irish foods, so it's no surprise that Findus Crispy Pancakes top many Irish people's list as their favourite food they ate when they were young (Angel Delight is another; see page 8).

But in 2016, when it was revealed that horsemeat was being used in products purporting to be beef, Findus pulled all its frozen products and dissolved the brand in the UK and Ireland (Hayward 2016). Even before the scandal, Findus beef lasagne products were found to contain up to 100% horsemeat (Neville 2013). Bird's Eye (owned by Nomad Foods, which owned Findus) now sells the crispy pancake range with some new fillings, such as mozzarella.

034
Fish 'n' chips

Not all fish served in Ireland comes with chips, but the combination is probably the first one that comes to mind (other than fish fingers) when you ask many Irish people about fish. Though we are not a nation of fish lovers, we do love battered, deep-fried food. I fondly remember fish 'n' chips in Jackie Lennox's chip shop (established in 1951) during my student days in University College Cork, when the fish 'n' chips were still wrapped in newspaper (which is less and less common nowadays).

Did you know that Italians brought fish 'n' chips to Ireland? I know what you're thinking: Italians and chip shops in Ireland? Surely that's a myth. But the next time you pass through a small Irish town, note the names of the chippers: Mario's, Romero's, Romayo's.

While Leo Burdock may claim to be Dublin's oldest chipper (operating since 1913), it certainly wasn't the first. Italian chippers date back to the 1880s, even though the golden era was around the 1950s. Interestingly, almost all the chipper families come from the same district of six villages in the Casalattico and Valle di Comino municipalities in the province of Frosinone in the Lazio region in Southern Italy.

According to the Irish Traditional Italian Chippers Association (for those of you who didn't know we had one), there are over 200 Irish-Italian chippers in Ireland. There is even a documentary on the subject called *Chippers* by Nick Tropiano.

Eating fish 'n' chips on plastic furniture as the summer suns sets encapsulates all that is great about the Irish food story.

o 3 5

Fish fingers

A fish finger sandwich is in the pantheon of Irish food for many of us who grew up in the 1970s and 1980s in Ireland. You simply couldn't get better than these frozen little cod sticks.

Fish fingers, along with Donegal Catch, saved a generation of us from choking on fish bones (I jest, of course). From independence in 1922 up until the late 1980s, fish in Ireland was associated with fasting, penance and misery. Fridays meant pieces of overcooked, floured, bony whiting – the act of eating it was more a labour than a pleasure. Fish fingers, on the other hand, were a godsend. Along with Findus Crispy Pancakes, they added a little colour to those grey days of pre-Celtic Tiger Ireland.

Of course, the TV advertising helped us enjoy them more. Captain Bird's Eye, a stolid adventurer of the open seas, was my hero. Who wouldn't want to eat his fish fingers? These food heros of my youth (Tony the Tiger was another) helped us become a little more modern by cooking and eating their processed foods. All the same, I remember fish fingers fondly, as do many Irish people.

Fish fingers emerged in the UK around 1900 and really took off during and after World War Two due to other food restrictions. However, it wasn't until 1955 that the frozen fish finger appeared. The frozen fish finger was invented by an American called Aaron L. Brody (who called it a 'fish stick'). Before cod or other white fish such as pollock became the standard, herring or salmon was often used. To make fish fingers, minced fish is frozen in 7.5kg blocks, then cut into 3-inch-long rectangular pieces and crumbed.

Fish fingers were not only a great teatime treat (the evening meal), they were also delectable in a well-buttered sandwich. We do like putting things between buttered bread in Ireland (*see also* 'Crisp sandwich', page 54).

036

Garlic

My parents told me that the first time garlic came into our house was after I stared working in Donatello's Italian restaurant in Maynooth in the mid-1990s, when my father would make garlic bread for us. This is in keeping with my theory of the Italianisation of Irish food following the success of the Irish football team in Italia '90. But where was all the garlic before then?

Wild garlic has been in Ireland for over 10,000 years. A 9th-century poem mentions 'garlic with May butter' as a cure for all disease. So when did we as a nation go off garlic? Was it during the long 20th century of independence and isolation? We've never been afraid of leeks, though, which are in the same family as garlic. Leek and potato soup is a common Irish country soup.

Like olive oil, garlic in early-20th-century Ireland seems to have been used as a panacea for all sorts of ills. According to Monica Sheridan, writing in *The Art of Irish Cooking* (1965), her parents used a concoction of garlic and whiskey for ailments such as sore tonsils, stomach aches and high temperatures. The 'nauseating brew' of whiskey and garlic was poured down the patient's throat in the hope that they would get better. Animals were also given the strange brew, and it 'occupied about the same place in our household as penicillin', according to Sheridan (1965: 117). Perhaps this is why so many Irish people were so opposed to garlic in food. (Interestingly, there are many recipes in Sheridan's book that include garlic, from shellfish soup to boiled leg of lamb with parsley sauce.)

Most garlic available in Ireland nowadays is imported, usually from China or Spain. There are, however, a few great garlic producers in Ireland, from Taylor's of Lusk to Drummond House in Louth. Drummond House, who also grow asparagus, grow four different heritage varieties of garlic as well as garlic scapes. Their endeavours to grow garlic in Ireland stand at the vanguard of its production.

o37
Ginger

We Irish are partial to ginger. It's in many of our sweet things, from biscuits and cake to other baked goods. It might not look Irish, but it defiantly is.

As with other spices such as cinnamon, nutmeg and mace, ginger goes back to the arrival of the Normans, who had a penchant for spices as well as dried fruit. Perhaps powdered ginger contributed a little bit of warmth to this cold country. How could a flavour that originated halfway across the world (possibly India) come to represent an aspect of Irish food?

The word *ginger* derives from the Sanskrit word *srngaveram*, which means 'horn' or 'antler', and refers to the way in which the root grows underground, as it is a rhizome that spread out in all directions.

The first literary reference to ginger comes to us from China around 200 BC, when it was used for medicinal purposes. We had to wait another 500 years for it to get to Europe, when the Romans listed it as a taxable commodity. The Romans made teas and wine with ginger (ginger wine was popular in Ireland in the 19th century) and preserved the roots in honey or spread it on meat. Throughout the Middle Ages, the ginger trade remained in the hands of Arab merchants travelling to Europe along the so-called Silk Road.

Gingerbread (which is actually more of a cake than a bread) was popular in the past and was sold at 'country markets and fairs and given to children as a treat' (Mahon 1991: 75). In her book *The Little Girls*, Elizabeth Bowen (1964) describes a scene where 'mothers unpack scones and potted meat sandwiches or cut up gingerbread.' Though the novel is set in England, Bowen was born in Dublin and wrote much about the Irish Big House tradition.

Gingerbread was usually made with treacle, brown sugar, preserved and ground ginger and plenty of sultanas and raisins. It's a beautiful example of the fusion of traditional Irish baking with 'exotic' ingredients.

038

Goose

Not too long ago in Ireland – a couple of hundred years at most – late September and early October was marked by roasting a goose. The goose would be stuffed with potatoes, then roasted over a turf fire. Michaelmas goose, as the tradition became known, was supposed to signify prosperity for the year ahead. The landlord would often be presented with the cooked goose along with the rent for that quarter.

In the days before turkeys were eaten in Ireland (they didn't arrive until 1550), goose was also a staple around Christmastime because a goose born in spring would be the perfect size by then. Christmas goose differs from Michaelmas goose in terms of what the goose would have been fed. Christmas goose was always finished on wheat as opposed to only grass. This would have made it fatter, which in turn means it would have fed more people. The goose would have been cooked over a turf fire with dumplings made with suet added to the pot half an hour before the goose was ready. In his 19th-century Irish novel *Knocknagow* (1879), Charles J. Kickham wrote of a young farmer who 'partook of boiled goose in his own house on an average of once a week ... the goose was always dismembered before it was put into the pot with the dumplings.'

The importance of geese in the past can be seen in Irish-language place names such as *Gort na gCadhan* ('Field of Brent Geese') in Co. Galway and *Inis Gé* ('Goose Island') in Co. Mayo. In terms of folklore, the goose appears often in Irish stories and legends. Because of their migratory patterns, many Irish people believed they were lost souls doomed to wander forever over the earth.

On a side note, the term 'wild geese' was used to refer to people who bravely left Ireland to fight with the French against the British on the European mainland in the 19th century. Many Irish wine houses in Bordeaux are collectively called by this name as well.

039

Gooseberries

Before I was born, my grandma grew gooseberries in her back garden. I never knew this growing up. Her back garden was always finely manicured whenever I spent time there as a boy. We even played croquet on the lawn. When I visited her in Mount Merrion in Dublin, I often wondered if I had been suddenly and mysteriously transported to another country, namely, England. Was my grandma an aspiring Anglo-Irish lady or did she just disagree with the way in which the Irish perceived themselves?

It was a different food story over in Bray with my nana. There, I felt truly Irish amid the squalor and the burnt sausages. But I suppose that's the problem with being Irish: our opposite is English (even though that's another myth; there is no 'opposite' to any country).

So what has all this got to do with gooseberries? I suppose the absence of fruit and vegetables in my grandma's garden signified it was no longer necessary to grow your own: the supermarkets had arrived (in 1966, to be exact). Another milestone in the Irish food story.

In her book *Irish Traditional Food* (1983), the grand dame of Irish food, Theodora FitzGibbon, included a recipe for gooseberry and fennel sauce for mackerel. The sauce dates from 1778 and represents an insight into the food story in Ireland during the 18th century, with its bold flavours and European influence. Gooseberry bushes were widely planted in gardens for medicinal purposes as well as for eating.

My favourite way to prepare gooseberries nowadays is to preserve them in salt for a few months and then use them with fish, such as smoked salmon, grilled mackerel and poached turbot. The sour, saline nature of the resulting gooseberries cuts through the richness of the fish.

Food writer Dee Laffan recalls how for her, the Wimbledon tennis tournament meant one thing: gooseberries.

My favourite part was making the jam. We would help wash the gooseberries, carefully discarding any branches or leaves. Sometimes we were allowed to stir the gooseberries as they simmered in water on the Aga in the kitchen. And we would help out with the jarring too. For gooseberry jelly, we would tie a large muslin cloth on the backs of two chairs opposite each other. We would put a steel bath underneath the stretched cloth. The mixture was poured into the cloth and it would drip into the bath below. This was jarred and produced a smooth, clear jelly.

Each year, I still welcome gooseberry season if only to pickle some of these sour delights to enjoy them during the rest of the year. Gooseberries can also be preserved in sugar syrup if you want to use them for sweet treats, such as Irish chef Vanessa Greenwood's gooseberry crumble.

040

Gur cake

Was gur cake the first no-waste cake? Originating in Dublin, gur cake is also known as donkey's gudge in Cork. A similar confection called Chester cake exists in Cheshire, England. The cake is an interesting combination of a pastry shell filled with a mixture of leftover (or rather, 'recycled') cake or breadcrumbs with dried fruits, sugar or treacle, and plenty of spices.

The *gur* in the name probably comes from the word *gurrier*, which is Irish slang for 'a ruffian.' As a cheap cake made from leftovers, gur cake could be afforded by children skipping school. This led to the term *gurrier* for the skiving children and *being on the gur* as the act of skipping school. In his book *Gur Cake and Coal Blocks* (1976), historian Éamonn Mac Thomáis regards gur cake as symbolic of the working-class areas in Dublin.

Gur cake is still a common sight around Ireland, where it's sold in bakeries in characteristic slabs. According to Dublin cookery writer Honor Moore, pieces of gur cake were called 'depth charges' in the 1940s, perhaps because of their density and weight and thus the way in which they evoked the bombs of World War Two (Allen 1995: 297).

In 2014, Irish journalist Caitríona Redmond called for gur cake to be granted EU Protected Designation of Origin (PDO) status as one of Ireland's unique foods:

> What I love about this cake is that it uses up leftovers and doesn't leave a bit of waste from baking a cake. I love that it is traditional, it harks back to harder, more frugal times, and that it just goes to show the ingenuity that people had to make food stretch further. Gur cake is a traditional Irish food. How on earth somebody in Dublin hasn't started the process to get EU Designated Status for gur cake, I just don't know.

041

Hay

Baking a celeriac in hay might not seem like a revolutionary or historical thing, but it is both. The Normans in Ireland boiled hams in hay and water. The tannic quality in hay not only added an earthy flavour but helped preserve the ham for longer. Ancient farmers stored their vegetables in hay boxes; that way, they could have fresh vegetables months after they were picked. Kept in a cool, dark, dry place, the hay would keep them from rotting.

As well as cooking ham in hay, many tribes in Ireland would roast lamb with hay or even wrap the lamb in hay before cooking it in water. The Neolithic *fulacht fia* (burned mounds) may have been used for pit cooking. Large cuts of meat wrapped in hay and slowly simmered in a pit of water heated with hot stones would have fed many people.

While *fulacht fia* have been proven to work for cooking, this does not tell us the whole story. The only known written source dates to the 17th century, so the jury is still out. At one of our Food on the Edge events, beer was prepared in a *fulacht fia* by cooking barley in a trough with the addition of hot stones to show that it was possible to do this using ancient technology. They also have been used for washing, so perhaps they were multifunctional – bathe, beer, lamb, in that order.

Though it may seem that we are light years away now with our rosemary and garlic, a quick search on the internet reveals that many chefs are still baking lamb with hay. Dress your lamb leg with extra-virgin rapeseed oil and sea salt. Put it on a few handfuls of hay in a suitable oven dish, then put more hay on top. Make sure the lamb is at room temperature before you put it in the oven. Roast for 90 minutes, then rest for 30 minutes. The resting is just as important as the cooking. While it's resting, baste the leg with the residual liquid left in the bottom of the dish (a wonderful mixture of hay and fat).

This dish is beautiful to serve straight to the table in front of your family or friends. Don't forget to give them the history lesson about cooking with hay!

o42

Honey

Ireland has long been known as 'the land of milk and honey.' For folklorist Bríd Mahon, Ireland's association with milk and honey derives from the fact that both of these foodstuffs have been abundantly available here since the 'earliest times' (Mahon 1991: 79).

Up until the introduction of cane sugar (which the Normans did on a small scale centuries before it was commonplace), honey was the only sweetener available in Ireland and was a vitally important foodstuff. In addition, from the outset of honey production in Ireland, rent and tributes could be paid in honey.

Honey, as well as honeycomb, was collected in large barrels. As well as being used in cooking, pure honey was also used as a dipping sauce for meat and fish (Mahon 1991: 80). Honey cakes were also popular at medieval Irish banquets.

Honey is also the main ingredient in mead, an ancient Irish alcoholic drink made with honey, water and aromatic plants. In the 12th-century food epic *The Vision of MacConglinne*, mead is described as 'the relish of noble stock,' while the banqueting hall at Tara (the seat of the High Kings of Ireland) is referred to as the 'house of the mead-circuit' (Hickey 2018: 272).

A medieval drink called braggot was also made by fermenting ale and honey together (Mahon 1991: 22). Many monastic settlements brewed their own mead, braggot and ale on site, though tonsured monks were only given half as much ale as their lay brothers.

To make honey, you need bees. There is mention of beekeeping and the production of honey in the Brehon Laws. Beekeeping has been practised in Ireland for close to 1,500 years. Honeybees were said to have been brought to Ireland from England by a monastic order. Legend has it that Saint Modomnóc brought bees to Ireland from Wales in the early 540s.

Ireland has long been known as 'the land of milk and honey'.

°43
Hot cross buns

Of the many traditions associated with Easter in Ireland, the baking (or consumption) of hot cross buns may be the most intriguing. Although we may have forgotten most of the complex symbolism that comes with them, this does not stop us from enjoying them.

Traditionally, the hot cross bun marked the end of Lent and different parts of the bun have different meanings. The cross represents the crucifixion of Jesus and the spices signify the spices used to embalm him.

The origin of the hot cross bun goes back to medieval times, at least as far back as the 14th century. Seemingly, in 1361, a monk in St Albans developed a recipe called an Alban bun and distributed the bun to the local poor on Good Friday to alleviate their suffering.

The first definitive record of hot cross buns comes from a London street cry:

> Good Friday comes this month, the old woman runs
> With one or two a penny hot cross buns.

This 'cry' appeared in *Poor Robin's Almanac* in 1733. The line 'One a penny, two a penny, hot cross buns', which we all knew as children, appears in the nursery rhyme 'Hot Cross Buns', first published in the *London Chronicle* in June 1767.

Hot cross buns contain spices and dried fruit that originate far from Ireland. We forget how much the spice trade has impacted our food history. While these ingredients would have once signified wealth and prestige, they now remind us of how open our country has become to international food trends throughout the centuries.

°44

Ice cream

It was far from crème anglaise or gelato that we were reared. Growing up, our ice cream was a block of HB cut into six or eight portions, then sandwiched between two shop-bought wafers. Blocks of ice cream were good for large families with six or more children, which was most families in Ireland in the 1980s. The best medicine when we were young was a scoop of vanilla ice cream and flat 7up. Another Irish favourite was an ice cream float with Coca-Cola or red lemonade.

HB ice cream goes back to 1926, when the Hughes brothers set up an ice cream parlour at their dairy at Hazelbrook Farm in Churchtown, Dublin. Television adverts of the 1980s declared HB the 'two letters [that] spell Ireland's favourite ice cream.'

HB wasn't the only show in town, though. There was also Valley Ice Cream, which was based out of Thurles, Co. Tipperary. Their 1980s TV advertisement with the 'big red fridge' is so sexualised that I wonder now how it made it past the censors. Leadmore Ice Cream was another small ice cream manufacturer that was based in Cork.

Growing up in Ireland, there was an inordinate number of ice creams in the shop freezer: Funny Feet, Fat Frogs, Loop the Loop, Choc-ice, Brunch and Cornetto, to name just a few. However, many of these brands have been overshadowed by the introduction of ice creams such as Magnum and Ben & Jerry's.

Irish ice cream makers Murphy's are fighting back against this global trend by serving delicious ice creams in their small shops around the country with flavours that nod to tradition, such as brown bread ice cream and Dingle sea salt ice cream.

The 99 is another legendary ice cream, served mostly during the summer in Ireland. A 99 is an ice cream cone made with soft-serve vanilla ice cream into which a Flake (a stick of chocolate) has been added.

Food often breaks free of its dietary value and becomes an act of love.

·045

Irish stew

Food often breaks free of its dietary value and becomes an act of love. For me, that was my mother's Irish stew. It's the perfect example of the comforting and affective power of food.

Traditionally, Irish stew was made with the neck of the mutton. Lamb would never have been used in the past, as the animal had too much value in terms of its wool, milk, yogurt and cheese.

'If a superior stew is wanted, use loin chops or those from best end of neck,' says the book *Cookery Notes*, an Irish government cookery book first published in 1924 (Department of Agriculture 1924). Included with the neck would be potatoes, onions and parsley. Carrots, turnips and pearl barley would often be added, though for 20th-century food writer Theodora FitzGibbon, 'the pure flavour is spoilt' if they are used (1968: 55). FitzGibbon also rails against the stew being 'too liquid.' She writes, 'A good Irish stew should be thick and creamy, not swimming in juice like soup.' Elsewhere, FitzGibbon refers to Irish stew as 'likely one of the oldest Irish recipes in existence' (1983: 117).

For food writer Florence Irwin, Irish stew was linked to the class structure that existed between the occupants of the Big House and the locals who worked the land and lived in little 'cabins':

> This dish originated in the Irish cabin. In it utensils were scarce – a frying pan, a griddle, a kettle and a potato pot sometimes constituting the entire cooking apparatus. When a pig or sheep was killed at the 'big house' the griskins, spare-ribs, or scrag end of the neck of mutton were shared with the peasants. Having limited vessels and more limited experience, the potatoes were peeled when meat was used, otherwise they were boiled in their 'jackets'; and meat, potatoes with onions were put in the pot, covered with water and all boiled together. So Irish stew was made, and without much change has remained a popular dish to this day (Irwin 1949: 70).

Meanwhile, Dorothy Cashman and John Farrelly (2021) present the history of the dish from 'its emergence from painful association with subsistence living to a confident place in the pantheon of Irish cuisine.' They ask the pertinent question: 'Do the recipe and the dish exist as a commodity unto themselves or alongside some totemic idea of Irishness, and if so, what has shaped that idea and how has it continued to be shaped to the present day?' (Cashman and Farrelly 2021: 81)

There are as many variations of Irish stew as there are families in Ireland. It means different things to different people over the centuries it has been made. Though there is historical and social continuity between my act of making Irish stew and the act of someone from the 18th century making it, the meaning of that moment is not the same.

American food writer Colman Andrews calls Irish stew 'the chili con carne, the paella, the tandoori chicken of Ireland – the emblematic dish, that seems (rightly or wrongly) to define an entire culture' (Andrews 2009: 165). Perhaps we should appreciate it more. Can you imagine a national food festival for Irish stew like the many festivals they have to honour paella in Spain?

The oldest manuscript mention of 'Irish mutton stew' is found in the Inchiquin Papers in the National Library of Ireland (c. 1753), while the oldest known recipe in print appears in Eliza Melroe's *An Economical and New Method of Cookery; Describing Upwards of Eighty Cheap, Wholesome, and Nourishing Dishes*:

> Take fat mutton chops, any quantity, for example, two pounds; potatoes from four to six pounds, washed and scraped; onions or leeks, a proportionate quantity; pepper and salt a sufficiency; stew the above with a small quantity of water, in a vessel covered. Note – it makes a very cheap, wholesome, nourishing dish, which I hope every family will be acquainted with, and this intimation rendered unnecessary – On the same principle, legs of beef, ox-cheek, or the fat sinewy parts of meat may be cooked (Melroe 1798: 58).

Interestingly, according to FitzGibbon in her book *The Food of the Western World* (1976), 'Irish stew was undoubtedly made, not with lamb or mutton, but with young male kid which was both lean and tender.'

Even though it is made less and less often in households and restaurants these days, Irish stew nonetheless stands in an indisputable position in relation to the idea of Irish food and its story.

046
Jacob's cream crackers

Jacob's remains at the forefront of Irish food consciousness. For many Irish people, freshly buttered Jacob's cream crackers and a cup of tea was tantamount to a meal. There were always crackers in the press when you came home from school. Sealed in an airtight plastic box, they could remain 'fresh' nearly forever, a failsafe when there was no more bread left in the house. They were regularly eaten with ham, cheese and butter stuffed between two crackers. I also have vague memories of adding grass to my butter crackers to see that it tasted like. Such are the taste explorations of an Irish child.

The cracker was the brainchild of James Haughton. It was first produced commercially by William Beale Jacob and entered the Irish market in 1885. Originally called 'west coast cracker', with a dubious image of a woman in a bathing suit on the beach on its packaging, the crackers were soon rebranded and became the iconic 'cream crackers' that every Irish household knows.

Jacob's cream crackers are easily identified by their distinctive 'dock and prick' pattern, which consists of small holes and perforations on the surface. These holes prevent the crackers from puffing up too much during baking, resulting in their iconic crisp, flat texture.

Interestingly, the Jacob's factory on Bishop Street, Dublin, was one of the buildings occupied by rebels during the Easter Rising of 1916.

In 1985, when Jacob's cream crackers turned 100 years old, the company was producing 2,500 crackers a minute.

Jacob's also made biscuits that were central to the Irish food story of my youth. The four big players were fig rolls, Mikados, Kimberleys and coconut creams. The latter three were equivalent to the holy trinity itself. Television advertisements made these biscuits rock stars in our eyes. We all wanted to eat them. We would often check whose parents had the most Jacob's biscuits and make sure to call over to their house for a cup of tea.

° 4 7
Jambons

The jambon is a curious Irish pastry made from ham, cheese and puff pastry that is usually sold in delis throughout Ireland. The Irish ate 20 million of them in 2020 alone. Does that mean they are the most popular food in Ireland? I'm not sure, but they may well be.

A jambon has nothing to do with a *jambon-beurre*, the famous French sandwich made from a baguette that's sliced open, spread with butter and filled with ham that's so popular, 3 million are sold daily in France. But it seems that the jambon did originate in France, where they are called *paniers feuilletés au jambon et au fromage* ('ham and cheese puff pastry baskets'). They arrived at much the same time as Cuisine de France baguettes and have become a staple at petrol stations, deli counters, supermarket 'bakeries' and just about everywhere else.

A jambon and the breakfast roll were the breakfasts of choice in the Celtic Tiger era for people on the move. Like the baguette, it signalled 'Frenchness', which in the 1990s was better than Irishness. Out with the porridge and the full Irish, in with the hand-held jambon. As Roland Barthes (1997: 28) writes in his essay 'Toward a Psychosociology of Contemporary Food Consumption', 'Food serves as a sign not only for themes, but also for situations; and this, all told, means a way of life that is emphasized, much more than expressed by it. To eat is a behaviour that develops beyond its own ends'.

The ham and cheese jambon was our way of escaping a food tradition that we had received from our parents and grandparents. Little did we know that this food tradition was actually much grander than we had been told. Though our fascination with the jambon continues, its place in the wider story of Irish food is now better understood – or at least I hope it is.

A jambon and the breakfast roll were the breakfasts of choice in the Celtic Tiger era for people on the move. Like the baguette, it signalled 'Frenchness', which in the 1990s was better than Irishness. Out with the porridge and the full Irish, in with the hand-held jambon.

048

Lamb

Lamb enters into our food consciousness in the spring. We cook it for Easter dinner, then we go back to eating beef and chicken with the occasional piece of fish. But spring lamb truly comes into its own in terms of flavour and size around August. By October, the lambs (still under a year old) have matured and grown from eating our beautiful grass, gorse and heather. Autumn is actually the best time to eat lamb in Ireland. Think Irish stew with barley and potatoes; roast lamb with rosemary and hay; lamb skewers with autumn courgettes; and rack of lamb with freshly foraged hazelnuts.

To understand our historical relationship to sheep in Ireland, we could look at the ways in which lambs were generally reared for their wool and milk as opposed to their meat (unless you were wealthy). As Regina Sexton observes in *A Little History of Irish Food* (1998: 36), 'Lamb and fattened young wethers were considered a delicacy from early medieval times and were demanded as food rents by the aristocratic classes. Sometimes, if a young animal died through misadventure, then lamb featured as an unexpected treat on the plates of the small to middling farmer.'

This may explain why mutton became popular among the native Irish over time, as older animals may have been killed towards the end of their life. Growing up, our Irish stew was always made with mutton, as lamb was simply too expensive. Most lamb sold today in Ireland is actually hogget (which means it's over a year old).

However, in the not-so-distant past a lamb would have been killed as a sign of hospitality. In his book *Pococke's Tour of Ireland in 1752*, Richard Pococke (1891: 92) observed this practice of offering lamb to visiting guests: 'The people in this Country are very hospitable, if you cannot stay to have a sheep killed they offer Ale a dram, Eggs and butter, and the woman of the house sits at the table and serves you.'

049
Lasagne, coleslaw &
chips

Growing up in Maynooth, Co. Kildare, my mother did most of the cooking, but lasagne was one of my father's go-to dishes. 'Come home, your father is making lasagne', was all she needed to say.

While a lasagne may not seem radical to a generation of children raised on Italian food and cheap flights to Venice and Rome, this dish marked my childhood like a branding iron in terms of innovation. When I was writing *The Irish Cookbook* (McMahon 2020), the editor asked me for some of my family recipes. Among many others, such as carrot cake and shepherd's pie, I included a version of my father's lasagne. While the former were met with editorial approval, the latter was dismissed for not being Irish enough.

How long does something have to be in a country before it becomes part of its food culture? Many of us have a narrow definition of what national food is based on recent history. Where a dish comes from and how it travels are two different things. I'm not saying that lasagne is an Irish food, but it *is* part of the food in Ireland. The latter encapsulates change, while the former attempts to keep food stuck in some timeless, myopic tunnel of mythological Irishness. The truth resides somewhere in between.

While lasagne may not yet be a part of the Irish food canon, the combination of lasagne, chips and coleslaw is a distinctly Irish one, served in many restaurants and pubs around the country. Indeed, I have happy memories of devouring this dish on many occasions in Abbey Tavern on Gillabbey Street, with many a pint of Beamish to wash it down, when I was a student in Cork. If that's not cross-cultural fertilisation, I don't know what is. It single-handedly brings everything you think about a national food into question.

For Italians, the lasagne, coleslaw and chips combination is sacrilege. But you can't stop food from travelling. Carbs and creamy fat on top of creamy fat with more carbs – what could be better?

How long does something have to be in a country before it becomes part of its food culture? Many of us have a narrow definition of what national food is based on recent history. Where a dish comes from and how it travels are two different things.

050

Leeks

At first, leeks may appear inconsequential to the Irish food story. However, they were used a lot in Irish 'Gaelic' cooking. These leeks were most likely Babington leeks, which still grow wild in the West of Ireland. They are a much hardier leek than the contemporary cultivated kind and need a lot more cooking.

The Irish Seed Savers Association was founded by Anita Hayes to safeguard indigenous and heritage varieties of fruits and vegetables in Ireland. Their Musselburgh leek, which is a variety of leek grown in Ireland since at least 1834, is a hardly, reliable vegetable that suits the Irish weather.

Brotchán roy is a traditional Irish soup that uses leeks along with oats and milk. These three ingredients are central to much historical cooking on this island. Later Anglo-Norman recipes added spices, such as mace, nutmeg and black pepper. The inclusion of these ingredients represents a fusion of Irish and outside influences, which is a hallmark of much of the Irish food story.

References to *brotchán roy* appear in the 9th-century manuscript *The Monastery of Tallaght*, where it is described as a meal for the monks. Leek and potato soup is still popular in Ireland today, with many different variations. I like to add dillisk seaweed to mine, while others like to add vegetables such as celery or spices such as nutmeg. In an Armagh recipe included in Florence Irwin's cookbook *The Cookin' Woman: Irish Country Recipes* (1949), white pepper and white celery are included as well as fried croutons.

For Monica Sheridan, the white part of the leek was the 'swan's neck' and should be the only part that goes into a leek soup to make it a 'very gentle soup' (1965: 13).

051

Marmalade

When I was growing up in the 1980s and 1990s, marmalade was made in many homes. The writer John D. Sheridan, a columnist for the *Irish Independent* in the 1950s, called January 'marmalade time' (Allen 1995: 308), as January is when Seville oranges are in season. While this practice is not as popular as it used to be, many still do make it, including cafés and restaurants around the country. Every year we make it at Aniar, I find myself reflecting on the many people who have made marmalade in Ireland over the centuries. The gift of hospitality was channelled through marmalade-making, as most was given away to neighbours and visiting guests.

Many recipe collections from the 18th century include a marmalade recipe. Indeed, the oldest collection of recipes in Ireland, from the 1660s, has a cherry marmalade. In her book *Irish Traditional Cooking*, Darina Allen documents a long list of marmalades made in Ireland over the centuries, from grapefruit to lemon. A recipe from 1865 from Lough Rynn uses lump sugar and spring water and cuts the orange into 'small chips', which Allen reckons would take one person a whole day (Allen 1995: 309). My own version of marmalade that I included in *The Irish Cookbook* (McMahon 2020) contained peated whiskey for an additional earthy, smoky character.

An interesting steamed marmalade pudding, made with a suet batter and ginger, is included in Maura Laverty's *Kind Cooking* (1955).

While we may believe we are more sophisticated and superior than generations past, the fast pace of our present lives leaves us little time to appreciate the seasons, especially short ones such as Seville orange season, which lasts for only a few weeks each January.

The next time you make marmalade in January, reflect on the role it has played in the Irish food story – and of course enjoy it on a freshly baked scone with plenty of butter.

052

Meat

We have a long relationship with all types of meat in this country, from the prime cut to the offcuts, from beef fillet to beef burgers. Historically, the average Irish person ate a lot less meat than we do now. While many Irish people today might balk at the idea of a meat-free meal (even though vegetarianism is on the rise), eating meat every day is a relatively recent phenomenon. In the past, beef (or a roast chicken) was reserved for Sundays or other celebratory moments (Sexton 1998: 27). Anything that was left over was used in other dishes later on in the week, such as cottage pie (or shepherd's pie if it was leftover roast lamb).

A direct, tangible link to meat is, of course, local butcher shops and abattoirs. After the arrival of supermarkets in the 1960s, local butchers gradually began to close. Ray Colleran, of Colleran's Butchers (now closed), told me that there were once over 96 butcher shops in Galway. I imagine there are only a handful now, though Divilly's (established in 1927) and Herterich's (established in 1940) are still going strong.

Ruth Hegarty, a food policy consultant, researcher and commentator, shared the story below, which highlights the difference between buying meat from a butcher and a supermarket, especially if the butcher had its own abattoir, which many of them did.

> Getting up to Granny's house meant walking right through the butcher shop, along by the counter and then in by the big wooden butcher's block to the door at the back that opened onto the carpeted stairwell up to the house. If the shop was open, we would be greeted by our uncle and the other butchers as we trekked through, and Granny might be there herself behind the counter in the navy-and-white striped apron. I loved those aprons and those moments.
>
> On Sundays, the shop would be all cleaned down and empty. All that was left was that smell of sawdust and blood to remind

you of what went on there all week. It's a unique smell that would surely transport me back there in an instant, except there is no more sawdust on the floors of butcher shops these days. But I still remember the feeling of that smell in my nostrils. I loved it.

Through the door at the back of the shop, straight ahead if you didn't take the stairs, was another door that would take you out to the yard, and in the yard was the abattoir. In the absence of any kind of garden, that is where my younger sister and I would run around and play. Somehow, we weren't put off by the metal hooks hanging from the ceiling or the smell of the sheepskins piled high, waiting for collection. I never saw a live animal there. I suppose our visits from Galway to our granny all the way over in Dunlavin, Co. Wicklow were normally on weekends, so there was no killing happening. Not seeing live animals, I didn't think too much about their deaths. But we did know where we were and what it was, and we didn't seem to mind.

If it was a Sunday, we would go up the narrow, maroon-carpeted stairs along the short dark hall, peeking into the spare room with the made-up beds and Granny's room with her carefully laid-out dressing table, and into the living room that looked out and down onto the street, with an impossibly tiny kitchen attached. Over by the window, the round dark wood dining table would be laid out with ornate, old-fashioned, matching dinner service, lidded serving dishes and a gravy boat. Granny would serve roast beef, cooked in that tiny kitchen, with a rich meaty gravy and all the bits. She was a good cook. There would be dessert too, something old-fashioned served with custard. But for me, it was all about the meat we ate right above the spot where the animal had died – the meat she would bring by the many pounds in her little red suitcase every time she came up on the train to Galway for a visit.

There are still a few butchers with their own abattoirs, such as Brady's in Athenry, but they are few and far between in contemporary Ireland.

°53
Milk

I remember the day my brother and I challenged each other to drink a litre of milk each. There was no logic to it; we just wanted to see if it was possible. I remember when bottles of milk were delivered to our front door by a milkman. I remember collecting tokens for milk cartons (collecting them for what, I don't know). I remember drinking milk after eating fried bread and the way it made your mouth go like wax. I remember the first time I drank milk straight from a cow and thought I'd get sick. For John Creedon, 'a glass of cold fresh milk to wash down the last of a stew or bacon was usually marked with "*Ahh … bainne an bó breac*" (Ahh, the milk of the speckled cow)' (Creedon 2022: 122).

Before the potato, there was milk. If we had to find a key to unlock Irish cuisine over the centuries, it would revolve around dairy. Milk was often the difference between 'prosperity and poverty' (Mahon 1991: 84). Milk and grain in the form of a rough porridge sustained the Irish for thousands of years.

In his article 'Irish Food before the Potato', historian A.T. Lucas (1960) observed that dairy has played a vital role in Ireland since the first Neolithic farmers. Before 20th-century industrial agricultural production, most farmers kept a mix of dual-purpose cows (Shorthorn and Friesian) for both dairy and meat. Most milk was produced domestically and used in the family home.

Butter was a valuable commodity, so it was usually sold (or used to pay rent or taxes) and rarely eaten by all. Every farmhouse churned their own butter, and the diversity of butter was outstanding in terms of what is available today. The skim milk left after the fat was removed from the milk was fed back to the animals or allowed to sour and became buttermilk (page 95).

This cycle of dairy farming dominated Ireland for thousands of years. Milk products were referred to as *bán bhia* ('white meat'), and because

Before the potato, there was milk. If we had to find a key to unlock Irish cuisine over the centuries, it would revolve around dairy.

of the role cattle played in the economy, their 'red meat' was seldom eaten except at feasts or special occasions.

Many milk products surfaced in Irish food history, from sour and ropy milk to buttermilk and cheese. It is fair to say that after the potato, milk was one of the most important foodstuffs in Ireland. Bríd Mahon observes in her book *Land of Milk and Honey* (1991: 84) that no other foodstuff 'was the subject of so many customs, traditions and superstitions.'

Of the many milks, there were *treabhantar* (fresh milk mixed with buttermilk) and *bainne clábair* (thick sour milk), not to mention the many versions of butter, curd and cheese that were made with milk. In 1690, a British visitor to Ireland noted that the natives ate and drank milk 'above twenty several sorts of ways and what is strangest for the most part love it best when sourest' (J. Stevens 1912). Sour milk and buttermilk were favourite drinks and were added to potatoes, cabbage and seaweed as a complete meal.

Goats and sheep were also kept for their milk. Though mostly used in cheese-making, the milk of these animals was also an important addition to other foods, such as porridge. Keeping sheep was cheaper than keeping a cow, so the custom of sheep's milk often emerged in poorer places or places that were not suitable for keeping cattle, such as mountainous regions. A new tradition of sheep's milk, cheese and yogurt has emerged in recent years in Ireland, particularly in the West. Velvet Cloud sheep's yogurt, produced in Claremorris, Co. Mayo, is probably the best representation of this new tradition.

Buttermilk

Long ago, buttermilk was a refreshing drink drunk by many. During harvest time, workers would quench their thirst with a mug full of buttermilk. During turf-cutting time, people would leave their buttermilk in the bog to keep it cool. Before the arrival of tea, a cup of buttermilk, straight from the churn, would be offered to visiting guests.

A glass of buttermilk was said to be good for a hangover and it was always in plentiful supply the day after weddings and wakes (Mahon 1991: 88). It was also used as a facewash to improve young ladies' complexions.

Buttermilk is our lemon. Its beautiful acidity sends me into overdrive. Of course, it's not as acidic as a lemon or a lime; its pH is much softer. But it still does a wonderful job of cutting through fat or protein. I love combining it with fish, especially shellfish. Oysters and buttermilk? The first time I did this combination, people shrieked. Not literally, but enough to say: are you mad? To me, it made sense. We are so used to serving lemon with oysters, but the combination of oysters and buttermilk is uniquely Irish and should be celebrated as such.

o 5 4

Mince pies

For many people, mince pies are the taste of an Irish Christmas. Even though mince pies originally contained meat, such as beef, mutton or venison, as well as a mixture of dried fruit, citrus peel, spices and suet, the word *mince* has nothing to do with meat – rather, it refers to the small size of the cut of the contents.

The origin of mince pies goes back to the Crusaders, who are said to have brought back the ingredients, such as dried fruits and spices. However, many of these ingredients were already in Europe, so the story seems apocryphal.

In the Middle Ages, the pies were often shaped into a manger to represent the crib of Christ. During the Victorian period, people began preparing the mixture ahead of time and the meat (but not the suet) gradually fell out of favour.

Nowadays, few people make their own mince pies. Chef Andy McFadden says his mother used to bake 'the most amazing mince pies at Christmas, which are legendary – she still won't give me the recipe. The pastry is absolutely incredible. On the last few days before Christmas, the kitchen is like a production line of mince pies that she would be rolling out and baking, then packaging really nicely to give to neighbours and family.'

Encapsulated in this observation is the act that many Irish people associate with baking. It's not only about making something for yourself; it's also about sharing with friends, family and neighbours. The gift of baking is a powerful thing that unites us as a community.

055
Mushrooms

Many Irish people harbour a bizarre hatred or strong dislike of mushrooms. Perhaps it was all those greasy full Irish breakfasts with sad, overcooked mushrooms that turned us off them. Or perhaps it's because they seem to reside somewhere between animal and vegetable, an organism that helps the trees to communicate with each other.

For too long, we have been a mushroom monoculture. Until recently, you would find only button mushrooms in the supermarkets. However, we seem to have turned a corner in relation to mushrooms, due in part to Brexit.

Garryhinch Mushrooms used to deal only in those white button mushrooms. Then Brexit happened and the Irish button mushroom market collapsed, so they stared to grow other types of mushrooms, such as shiitake, oyster and maitake, to name a few. While many of us here in Ireland still refer to these 'other' mushrooms as 'exotic' – indeed, the full name of Garryhinch is Garryhinch Wood Exotic Mushrooms – those in the know treat them more like recently arrived culinary immigrants. Five years ago, it was difficult to get Irish-grown shiitake mushrooms, but now you can get Garryhinch's mushrooms in supermarkets around the country. It's time we gave button and portobello mushrooms a break and moved into the 21st century in terms of mushrooms in Ireland.

While you never see a cloche anymore, even in restaurants, one 18th-century recipe serves mushrooms under a cloche. Butter, bread and mushrooms are alternately layered, then baked in an oven (FitzGibbon 1983: 41).

056

Mutton

It seems to be a growing trend that all mutton (and hogget too, for that matter) is labelled as lamb. I don't know if this follows US practice, where all sheep products are labelled lamb, or if something else has made us ignore the distinction. Is it to do with the simplification of our food culture, the reduction of every type to a single thing? Beef is beef, lamb is lamb. Except when it's not.

Traditionally, lamb is meat from a sheep that is less than one year old. Hogget is meat from a sheep that is more than one year old, while mutton is usually meat from a sheep that is more than three years old. I would guess most hogget is sold as lamb nowadays. It's a pity because the subtle difference is worth exploring. It's a larger animal with more developed meat, which to my mind is better. Spring lamb is a fatuous marketing tool. Most spring lamb arrives in the summer and in fact the best time to eat lamb is the autumn (*see also* 'Lamb', page 84).

Two memorable dishes that I came across in the National Library of Ireland archives were a shoulder of mutton with oysters (from Clonbrock House, Co. Galway, c.1753) and a lamb and oyster pie (from Fingall Papers, Co. Dublin, c.1740–60). You're not likely to come across this combination today. In 2018, cooking with British chef Adam Reid in Aniar, we brushed a roasting lamb saddle with blended oysters and the result was surprising, to say the least – like a sheep that had had a swim in the ocean.

Interestingly, one of oldest known written recipes attributed to 'Irish cooking' is a leg of mutton cooked '*à la mode d'Irlande*'. This recipe, as well as a duck and a 'peeled head of veal', were included in *Ouverture de Cuisine* ('*Opening the Kitchen*') by Lancelot de Casteau in 1604. Mutton and Ireland seem to have gone hand in hand over the preceding centuries. This was probably because eating lamb would have seemed counterintuitive because it could give you milk, wool, yogurt and cheese as long as it was alive.

A remarkable 18th-century mutton dish is included in Theodora FitzGibbon's *Irish Traditional Food* (1983: 115): 'For our feast there was prepared what here they call a "swilled *mouton*", that is, a sheep roasted whole in its skin, scorched like a hog. I never ate anything better; we sat on the grass, had a rock for our table and there was a great variety of good cheer, nothing was touched but the *mouton*.'

An 18th-century French traveller called Madame de Bovet who was critical of most of the food in Ireland did reserve some praise for the mutton, which she said was 'the only triumph of Irish cookery' (FitzGibbon 1983: 115).

While we have come a long way since then, finding mutton would be the biggest issue these days, as it has fallen completely out of favour. We often receive one or two a year from Bernard King of Connemara Mountain Lamb. Upon cooking, it doesn't seem to have that dreaded gaminess that I associated with lamb in my youth. Has the flavour of mutton changed over the decades or have Irish palates evolved to appreciate its pronounced flavour?

057

Nuts

Almonds

Though not native to Ireland, the Irish have had a penchant for almonds (in terms of recipes) since at least the 18th century. Indeed, this love of the almond goes back even further, to at least the arrival of the Normans in the 12th century. According to Meriel McClatchie, professor of archaeology at University College Dublin, one of the earliest mentions of almonds in Ireland is from medieval Cork, where almond stones were discovered in two amphora-type jars (Power 1928).

Almonds probably made their way to Cork by boat and were likely destined for a noble Anglo-Norman family due to how expensive they were. Almonds, as well as figs and walnuts, were available to buy in the market in Dublin in the 14th century (if you had the money, that is).

A recipe for watercress and almond soup, made with ground almonds, wild watercress and white pepper, dates to 1735 and is included in Theodora FitzGibbon's *Irish Traditional Food* (1983). What almonds, and this soup, tell us about Irish food is that we need to consider the fact that Ireland is an island inhabited by a diverse group of people who had different access to food over a long period. We cannot separate our indigenous and non-indigenous foods because we want the indigenous food to be more authentic. That is to say, *food in Ireland* is much more revealing than *Irish food* is about our food culture. Food history does not operate according to our desires. It has its own contingent and often chaotic pathways that we cannot control. The future of Irish food is a mixture of what resides inside and outside this island, the terms of its history and the people who continue to populate it. A bowl of almond and watercress soup with white pepper demonstrates this with every mouthful.

Hazelnuts

Most of the hazelnuts in the world come from Turkey. Irish hazelnuts are hard to find these days, though I know they grow well in the Burren in Co. Clare.

Anyone who has ever shelled a wild hazelnut or cobnut will appreciate the convenience of packets of shelled hazelnuts in the supermarkets. A bowl of roasted hazelnuts dressed with Newgrange Gold cold-pressed rapeseed oil and a sprinkling of smoked Achill Island Sea Salt is the Irish equivalent of those little bowls of spiced almonds you find in sunny Spain. I'd happily serve them to anyone and say, 'There you go – this is Irish food. This is our culture and our history.'

The remains of charred hazelnut shells have been found in many Irish Mesolithic sites, so the next time you sit down to a bowl of them, close your eyes and imagine you are part of an ancient Irish feast. Indeed, hazelnuts may have been the currency of exchange in Mesolithic Europe, not only as a food but also because the tree was used for many other practical purposes. The hazel tree itself occupies an important place in Irish mythology. W.B. Yeats wrote in his poem 'The Song of Wandering Aengus':

> *I went out to the hazel wood,*
> *Because a fire was in my head,*
> *And cut and peeled a hazel wand,*
> *And hooked a berry to a thread;*

Other ways to use freshly shelled and roasted hazelnuts are to grate them over a ham hock or chicken terrine or to combine them with the same weight in sugar and melt them together to make a simple praline, an old way of preserving hazelnuts in sugar for the winter.

Aside from wild hazelnuts, there are several Irish farmers growing them. Glenidan Farm is a small, family-run farm in Collinstown, Co. Westmeath that grows apples, aronia berries and sea buckthorn berries in addition to hazelnuts.

058

Oats

Oats have been a constant staple in the Irish 'Gaelic' diet and have been farmed in Ireland since at least 500 BC. They suited the inclement Irish weather and thrived in poor soil. Though a minor crop (in relation to wheat, barley and rye), they provided sustenance to pastoral folk.

Before the arrival of the potato in Ireland, oats and milk were an important part of the diet. In *A History of Ireland Written in the Year 1571*, Edmund Campion (2009) describes oatmeal and butter being combined to create a meal. Oats were usually eaten in the form of a gruel or porridge and were added to stews that were cooked slowly over open fires in a central hearth. 'A fair white porridge made with sheep's milk' is mentioned in the 12th-century poem *The Vision of MacConglinne*. Stirabout is an older name for porridge in Ireland.

Though porridge can be made with many different grains, such as barley and wheat, it is the dish that is most often associated with oats in the Irish imagination. As well as adding butter and buttermilk, honey, salt and sheep's milk could also be added to porridge. Medieval monks were known to garnish their porridge with all sorts of wild and cultivated fruits, from apples to blackberries.

Oats also went into bread and cakes, which contributed to the daily diet of the rural poor. And when other grains were in short supply, oats were occasionally used for making beer (though its reception does not seem to have been great).

The Irish oat cake (which is more of a biscuit) goes back to the Bronze Age in some form or other, but the modern version dates back only a few centuries. Oat cakes were probably the first 'bread' to be made in Ireland.

In the second letter of his book *Teague Land: Or a Merry Ramble to the Wild Irish*, John Dunton (1698) describes receiving oat cakes in Connemara along with butter, beef and mutton.

Traditionally, oat cakes would have been sweetened with honey before the arrival of sugar. Some recipes use lard instead of butter as well as treacle to darken the colour of the cake. Different regional varieties exist, from Donegal to Kerry. The cake is often baked more as a flat cracker. As with boxty, a pancake is sometimes made from the mixture.

Though the image of oats suffered in the 20th century due to their association with the poverty endured for many generations, they are now a feature on many menus and find their way into people's homes as a 'health food.'

° 5 9
Offal

The Irish never wasted any part of an animal. Indeed, you could say the same for most countries before the advent of industrial farming and supermarkets.

In James Joyce's *Ulysses* (1922), the character Leopold Bloom ate the inner organs of everything with relish. Was this out of love or necessity? I couldn't imagine eating Theodora FitzGibbon's kidney soup, which is made with ox or pigs' kidney's, a little sherry and some mace. Cow and sheep livers are the most popular in Ireland. Dusted with seasoned flour and fried quickly in butter and sage, it is a meal that is probably unknown to most people in modern Ireland.

Lamb's heart & other bits

In her book *Irish Traditional Food*, Theodora FitzGibbon describes a dish of stuffed lamb's heart as a 'good country dish [that] is gaining popularity again' (1968: 121). I'm not sure if FitzGibbon's remarks reflected reality or wishful thinking. You'd be hard pressed to find a lamb's heart in any butcher shop or supermarket nowadays.

When we first opened our restaurant Cava, we had lamb's heart stuffed with pork and chorizo on the menu. I remember a butcher's daughter refusing to eat it. We probably sold six to eight a week. Gradually, it fell off the menu.

Yet Antoniette O'Mahony in Galway remembers that roast sheep's heart was a quick midweek meal:

> One of my favourite meals was roast dinner and though not a regular occurrence, I used to be delighted when it was stuffed roast sheep's heart for dinner. This would never be a Sunday roast but a 'fancy' midweek meal. As a kid, I never fully understood or thought about the part of the animal that was going to be eaten – it was all just 'roast meat'. However, the

taste and texture of slow-roasted heart with onion stuffing, sewn up perfectly by my mam pre-cooking, was just divine. To this day, I can almost taste it. I do remember the hearts being really cheap to buy but took ages to cook. What was saved on the meat was most likely spent on electricity. I also loved eye bones in stews and used a tiny egg spoon to get all the marrow out.

Lamb's kidneys on toast was a popular breakfast dish in the 19th century, along with pan-fried lamb's liver. Padraig MacAdhastair remembers fried lamb tails, as does Gerry Costello. Costello says:

> Lamb tails were a delicacy enjoyed by our grandparents, our parents and generations before us. They were a much-sought-after food. In our house when I was young and my grandparents were still with us, there were never enough of them for me, thank God, so I never experienced eating lamb tails and I don't have the desire to start now. All the older generation enjoyed a 'good feed of lamb's tails' after docking the lambs took place.

Lamb tails were removed and then the remaining wool was burnt off. Costello recalls a 'foul-smelling smoke' as the tails were cooked over an open grill. They were eaten like ribs, though I don't imagine they were as tasty.

Steak & kidney pie

Steak and kidney pies began their life in the Anglo-Irish Big Houses before they became an economical way of filling out a steak pie to finally being turned into a processed tinned food.

For many Irish people, steak and kidney pie evokes a bygone era. During the lunch episode of James Joyce's *Ulysses*, several characters enjoy steak and kidney pie – a 'dinner fit for princes' – in the Ormond Hotel (Joyce 1922: 269). For Margaret Leahy, tinned steak and kidney pie brings back memories of her childhood.

Looking back at the TV adverts, especially the one where the recently married woman in the butcher shop is advised to buy a Fray Bentos steak and kidney pie instead of making one, I can see how it all went wrong in the Irish psyche. How this once-elaborate pie made with shoulder meat and ox or veal kidney became a convenience

I can see how it all went wrong in the Irish psyche. How this once-elaborate pie made with shoulder meat and ox or veal kidney became a convenience food demonstrates how we as a nation have turned many of our traditional foods into ultra-processed junk.

food demonstrates how we as a nation have turned many of our traditional foods into ultra-processed junk.

Denny, the famous Irish butcher who seemingly invented the rasher around 1820, also made a steak and kidney pie of their own for the Irish market.

Tripe

When I was a student at University College Cork, I often passed the old women cooking tripe at the famous O'Reilly stall that sold tripe and drisheen in the corner of the English Market. It looked beastly and it smelled even worse.

Tripe is the inner lining of a cow's stomach. It was once common in many European countries as well as the Middle East. Somehow it became a thing in Cork, along with drisheen, a sheep's blood sausage. Mentioned in the 12th-century poem *The Vision of MacConglinne*, by the 17th century it was widely available in the shops of Cork (Allen 1995: 138). Due to its bland nature, it was often heavily spiced. Tripe was combined with drisheen, which must have made for a gnarly teatime.

Tripe and onions is an old Irish dish and is mentioned in Oliver St John Gogarty's novel *Tumbling in the Hay*, published in 1939. Perhaps James Joyce was thinking of it when the character of Simon Daedalus proclaimed 'shite and onions' in *Ulysses* (Joyce 1922). The most common way to cook tripe was to poach it in milk with a lot of onions and spices, such as nutmeg or mace (more Norman influence). It would then be served with white sauce or baked in the oven with ham and breadcrumbs. As with pig's feet and collared pig's head, these are dishes of a different time, a different Ireland.

060
Olive oil

It's hard to imagine an Ireland without olive oil, but there was a time not too long ago when we never considered cooking with anything other than butter or some other animal fat.

Though Don Carlos began bringing olive oil to Ireland on a commercial scale in the late 1970s, Irish cookbooks written from the 1950s onwards by authors such as Monica Sheridan, Maura Laverty and Theodora FitzGibbon include recipes that use it. Yet my father, who grew up in Dublin at the same time these women were writing, told me that the only place you could buy olive oil was the pharmacy and that it was used to remove wax from blocked ears.

Perhaps it was with this difficulty of procurement in mind that made Monia Sheridan offer the reader the choice to use either olive oil or butter in her tomato sauce recipe in her book *Monica's Kitchen* (Sheridan 1963: 107). Yet Sheridan was no stranger to olive oil (or Italy), as can be discerned from reading her pages in the same book on spaghetti and pizza. This must have been at the vanguard of cooking in Ireland in the 1960s.

Was it de Valera's trade war with the British or simply Ireland's isolation that made it difficult to procure olive oil? Whatever the reasons, we can now happily cook with olive oil until the cows come home. As for trips to Spain and Italy (of which Sheridan enjoyed many), more of us can now experience them for ourselves thanks to cheaper air travel.

061

Onions

Onions go back as far as recorded history in Ireland does. They make up the backbone of much Irish food, from coddle to Dingle pies. In his book *Early Irish Farming*, Fergus Kelly (1997) observes that *cainnenn*, one of the most frequently mentioned vegetables in early Irish texts, refers to a type of onion used from the Middle Ages onwards.

Many recorded dishes of onions, such as baked onions or onions with bacon, cook the onions whole, to be served as a vegetable. According to the Irish food writer Theodora FitzGibbon, onion soup was said to cure all ills – even broken ribs! In contrast to French onion soup, which is brown, Irish onion soup is white due to the absence of caramelisation. In her book *The Cookin' Woman* (1949), Florence Irwin recommends scalding onions (blanching them in boiling water) to remove their astringent flavour.

The great Irish writer and satirist Jonathan Swift even penned a poem, 'Market Women's Cries', with three sections: one about apples, one on herring and one on onions:

> *Come, follow me by the smell,*
> *Here are delicate onions to sell;*
> *I promise to use you well.*
> *They make the blood warmer,*
> *You'll feed like a farmer;*
> *For this is every cook's opinion,*
> *No savoury dish without an onion;*
> *But, lest your kissing should be spoiled,*
> *Your onions must be thoroughly boiled:*
> *Or else you may spare*
> *Your mistress a share,*
> *The secret will never be known:*
> *She cannot discover*
> *The breath of her lover,*
> *But think it as sweet as her own.*

062

Packet soup

Growing up, I loved Knorr oxtail and tomato soup – especially after cycling home from school in the rain. But where was the oxtail in the soup? And how did they turn it into a powder?

Imagine my surprise when I found out that the word *ox* in the soup was more of a historical marketing strategy than an actuality. Not that there were no *tails* in my soup: it's just that they could come from any bovine. But cow tail soup just doesn't have the same ring to it.

It is said that oxtail soup was 'invented' in Spitalfields in London in the 17th century by French Huguenot and Flemish immigrants. This may be a stretch, though, as there are many older Asian equivalents. China, Korea and Indonesia all have oxtail soups that were made much earlier than the 17th century.

Campbell's first produced a tin of this tasty soup, then Knorr and Erin followed suit. Erin, who makes the famous Hotcup, started in 1963 and was bought by Campbell's in 2002.

If the supermarket shelves are any indication, we seem to love packet soup in Ireland. Irish food writer Dee Laffan fondly remembers that her father often combined the mixtures from different packets of dry soup to make his own custom 'Laffan blends' (Valencia, Laffan and Chin 2023: 4).

Although it's been years since I had one, many Irish men, women and children are still adding hot water to a packet of dry soup mix and relaxing into reverie.

o63

Pancakes

The night before Shrove Tuesday (Pancake Tuesday), my mother would make pancake batter. It was better, she said, if it rested overnight. There was never a truer word. The day after it's made, the batter is less glutinous, more digestible, lighter.

The excitement was almost palpable. I would cycle home from school eager to eat as many pancakes as possible. In our house, a pancake could have three toppings: lemon juice straight out of the Jif bottle (I don't think I saw a fresh lemon until I started working in an Italian restaurant when I was 15); jam, usually bought from the local shop over the road, though occasionally it could be a jar given by a neighbour or a relative (everyone seemed to make jam back then); or pure white Irish sugar sprinkled over the soft, pale yellow pancake. I often combined all three toppings on the one pancake – so much sugar, so much lemon juice (if you could call it that). I usually faltered after three. I didn't know it then, but this was my introduction to how acidity and sugar work together to make a balanced dish.

In her novel *Never No More*, published in 1942, Maura Laverty (2004) describes her own excitement while also pointing to the different ways pancakes were made around the country:

> I always looked forward to Shrove Tuesday and to Gran's pancakes, which were not made in the Kildare way with an ordinary batter of milk and eggs and flour. She made them as they make them in the West of Ireland, with grated raw potato. She got her recipe for boxty potatoes from her mother who was a Mary Kelly from Galway [...] The boxty pancakes were crisp little crumpet-like cakes that were eaten hot with butter and sugar as they came from the pan. Shrove Tuesday was unthinkable without boxty-on-the-pan. They were the fortune-tellers that gave you a glimpse of what the coming year held for you.

064

Pears

Apple orchards abound in Ireland, but it's only occasionally you'll come across an orchard of pears. There is no large commercial pear grower in Ireland. Pears take time to grow and fruit – anywhere between three and 10 years – but they can then fruit for hundreds of years, hence the saying 'plant pears for your heirs.' It is said there are 300-year-old pear trees in England still bearing fruit.

The Normans brought pear trees to Ireland. They were grown on many landed estates here for centuries. The Huguenots, who arrived in Ireland in the 18th century to escape persecution at home in France, grew pears, as well as apples and grapes (Hickey 2018: 225).

In addition to eating them raw, pears can be roasted, pickled and added to cakes and other desserts. Pear jam, served with cold meats and cheese, was also made in Ireland to accompany grand buffets in the past.

David Llewellyn produces a perry (pear cider) using the champagne method from his pears that he grows in Lusk in Co. Dublin, while Mark Jenkinson from Cockagee Cider in Co. Meath makes a dry, sparkling perry from Irish-grown pear varieties Plant de Blanc and Poire de Cloche.

It's a pity we don't plant more pear trees in Ireland. According to Andi Wilson, owner of the Westport-based specialist nursery Fruit and Nut, the best pear varieties to grow in Ireland are Conference, Concord and Doyenné du Comice. At Christmas or for birthdays, why not give the gift of a pear tree that they can watch grow, then gift in turn to the next generation?

o65

Peas

Peas were most likely first cultivated in Ireland in monastic settlements due to the care and attention needed to grow them – they would have been protected from Ireland's harsher weather in the walled gardens of the monasteries. Peas (and beans) were worth so much to people in the medieval period that they were included in the Royal Charter granted to New Ross in 1374 as a food that might be levied against.

Growing up in the 1980s, I never saw a fresh pea. Like corn, which came in a tin, peas came from a bag in the freezer. I have a vague memory of a television advertisement from the 1980s featuring lush green fields with just enough rain. 'Come home … to Bird's Eye country' sang the sweet voice.

My mother always overcooked peas, boiling them for many more minutes than they needed. Thankfully, I was never subjected to dried marrowfat peas, those gut-wrenching, gooey things. Though I am partial now to mushy peas with fish 'n' chips, perhaps it was the way we cooked marrowfat peas in Ireland that was the problem.

Marrowfat peas were traditionally accompanied by corned beef or pork. In Sara Power's manuscript book of 1746, there is a pea soup made with sorrel, spinach, black pepper, mace and lemon peel. For Theodora FitzGibbon (1986: 26), peas (fresh, frozen or dried) represented the 'most popular vegetable in Ireland.' A soup of dried peas made with the leftover bacon water is included in her collection. For fresh pea soup, FitzGibbon says to include the pods of the peas in the ham stock for additional flavour. This is a practice that we continue today to make a nice pea stock for many of the spring dishes in Aniar.

o66

Poitín

Poitín (anglicised as poteen or potcheen) is a potent Irish spirit made from potatoes or grains. Though it was outlawed in 1661, being illegal didn't stop its production, particularly in the West of Ireland.

In 1556, at parliament in Drogheda, it was decided that a licence was required of make, distil or sell alcohol. On top of that, in 1662 taxes on alcohol also came into effect in Ireland. This pushed many Irish farmers who made spirits underground.

On the Inishowen peninsula, poitín came to be known as 'mountain dew'. Several phrases associated with drinking, such as 'dead drunk' and 'waking the dead', come from people drinking too much poitín (Boyle 2023). American soldiers stationed in the North during World War Two were even warned about this illegal drink.

It took more than 300 years before poitín became legal again in 1997, with many illegal stills destroyed by the Guards over the years. There is some wonderful historic footage in the RTÉ archive of 'daring' police raids and an interesting bilingual radio documentary about poitín-making from 1976 called *Drop of the Craythur* by Pat Feeley.

Pádraic Ó Griallais is a sixth-generation poitín producer based in Connemara who represents the future of the drink. He continues an almost 200-year-old family tradition at the Micil distillery, which can trace its roots back to the mid-19th century. Because it was illegal for most of its existence, poitín is still not as popular as whiskey or gin but more distillers are now turning their attention to this unique Irish drink.

067

Pork

Pigs are not native to Ireland, though they were probably the first animal to be domesticated (or rather, semi-domesticated), allowed to roam wild in the native woods eating acorns and hazelnuts. They would have come over on boats with the first Neolithic farmers (Bardon 2008).

The pig appears in many early Irish tales, particularly ones about the Fianna (bands of warriors in Irish mythology). In these tales, wild pigs are often ferocious or enchanted. There are references to pigs in other texts too, such as *The Cattle Raid of Cooley* and *The Annals of Clonmacnoise* (1038).

Domestic pig farming emerged slowly and eventually replaced the pursuit of wild boar. As food historian Regina Sexton remarks, the keeping and feeding of pigs in the Middle Ages was 'exclusively women's work, and they fattened them up on a mash of milk and corn [...] improving their flesh prior to slaughter' (Sexton 1998: 45).

Even before the arrival of the potato (which increased the pig population, as they loved their spuds), the pig was vital to the Irish economy. November 11th (the Feast of St Martin) was a key date for slaughtering pigs. Many texts in the Brehon Laws concern themselves with the pig. In his essay 'Irish Food before the Potato', historian A.T. Lucas (1960) observed that laws indicated 'swine may sleep in a sty secured with four strong fastening by night and must have a swineherd with them by day'. In his 12th-century book *Topography of Ireland* (Giraldus Cambrensis 2000), Gerald of Wales observed that 'in no part of the world are such vast herds of boars and wild pigs to be found' than in Ireland.

In terms of varieties, the Greyhound pig (so-called because of its shape) is often cited. Both the Tamworth and Large White Ulster are a mix of the Greyhound and other native English varieties. Due to our desire for leaner pigs, the Large White became extinct in the 1960s. Most Irish pigs today are a mixed breed, a fusion of European and Asian varieties, though many smaller artisan famers are returning to heritage varieties with more flavour and fat. The difference between heritage pork varieties and their industrial equivalent is incomparable, hence the need to seek out these pigs and support their producers.

Bacon

Nearly every piece of pork in Ireland gets transformed into bacon in some manner or other, by which I mean it gets salted. This is not only down to taste preference but also because preserving fresh pork in salt gives it a longer shelf life and a deeper pink hue.

For most Irish people, bacon means rashers. The famous Irish playwright Brendan Behan said the Abbey (Ireland's national theatre) was the 'best-fed theatre company in the world because, every time there was a crisis in the kind of plays it put on, someone put on a pan of rashers' (O'Toole 2013). Rashers make the world go round, especially in Ireland. For poet Patrick Kavanagh, the 'fizz of rashers on a pan' was the answer to any empty stomach (O'Mara and O'Reilly 1993: 142).

At the outset of the Free State in 1922, bacon was one of our primary industries. Bacon ribs, alongside pig tails, were supplied to the local pub every Friday evening, according to Rick Higgins of Higgins Family Butchers in Sutton, to keep the punters thirsty for more drink. While we now munch on vegan 'bacon' fries in most pubs in Ireland, we would do well to remember the reality of our porky past.

Bacon & cabbage

While many Americans see corned beef and cabbage as the archetypal Irish dish, it's actually bacon and cabbage. As I said on page 20, bacon seems to have been replaced for a variety of reasons when this dish went Stateside. Though many famous Irish chefs have made their own 'lighter' versions over the years, the traditional slab of bacon and cabbage cooked in the bacon water (accompanied with a white sauce containing lots of parsley) would still whet the appetite of many an Irish man and woman if you were to set a plate of it in front of them. It's still a dish that brings much comfort to many Irish people. Perhaps the Kerry writer John B. Keane puts it best in his book *Strong Tea* (1963: 72):

> Lest the wrong impression be given, let me say at once that the type of bacon I have in mind is home cured. It has been hanging from the ceiling for months, and when you cut a chunk from it there is the faintest of golden tinges about its attractive shapeliness. When this type of bacon is boiling with its old colleague, white cabbage, there is a gurgle from the pot that would tear the heart out of a hungry man.

Keane remarks that the cooking of the bacon and cabbage produces 'an odour of such winning appeal'. From my own memoires, I'm not sure I would concur. I am still scarred by the smell of overcooked cabbage in murky bacon water.

Crubeens

Once up on a time, crubeens (pigs' feet) were served in pubs. Theodora FitzGibbon (1983: 127) calls them a 'country dish' that was usually served with 'brown soda bread and pints of stout'.

Like a freakish corn on the cob, you pick up the boiled trotter with both hands, bend your head down and apply your teeth to the bone, skin, gristle and the tiniest amount of meat. If you're looking for a truly Irish food experience, get yourself a pint of stout and a crubeen and find yourself a quiet corner in the pub. You won't forget it.

Ham

With so much sliced ham around nowadays, we forget that it was once a premier food of Ireland. Limerick was famous for its ham, bacon and sausages. Due to the production of bacon and ham there, Limerick became known as Pigtown, a tradition that stretched from the mid-19th century until Ireland joined the EU and the dynamic changed for pork producers in Ireland due to the availability of cheaper EU imports.

Limerick ham was famous for its smoky flavour, which was obtained from juniper berries. According to a recipe from 1779, hams would be smoked in chimneys over a fire 'of oak shavings [...] straw and one pound of juniper berries' for two to three days (FitzGibbon 1968:

75). Limerick ham travelled far and wide across the British Empire (O'Mara and O'Reilly 1993: 113). O'Mara's, which opened in 1839, was one of the most famous ham producers in Limerick. In fact, they were so famous they even had a factory in Russia (1891) and offices in Romania and London. Their hams were labelled 'Best in the World'.

With the cooking of hams mostly reserved for Christmastime for many of us now in Ireland, the demand is not what it used to be, especially with the younger generation. Each Christmas, many Irish ham producers bemoan the lax labelling of Danish hams (which are often sold as Irish) and the fact that ham can be produced in Ireland from pork that originates outside the country.

Ham hocks, once called 'poor man's ham', are witnessing a revival due to their less expensive nature. All the ham sandwiches we ever made in our café Tartare were produced with slow-cooked and shredded ham hock. Once you go hock, you'll never go back.

Ham & cheese sandwich

A good ham and cheese sandwich can define the nation where it is served: what type of bread, what type of ham, what type of cheese? Then you need to turn to other concerns: butter or mayonnaise, cucumber and/or tomato, wholegrain or English mustard?

The Irish love a ham and cheese sandwich at nearly every occasion. The meaning and value, and thus the taste, of food are always contingent on its circumstances. Many say the ham should be carved from the bone and that the cheese should be farmhouse, but more often than not, what you get is sliced pan, pre-sliced ham and ultra-processed cheese. We have the best and the worst ham sandwiches in the world in Ireland, though the best is not often defined as those that use better-quality ingredients and the worst aren't always the ones that use the cheapest ham and ultra-processed cheese.

I often bemoan those pre-packed ham and cheese sandwiches sold in every petrol station on the island, North and South. It's high time we called for a ham and cheese sandwich revolution, with regional varieties of ham and cheese and different breads. Can it really be so difficult? The food culture that resides behind the simple ham and cheese sandwich is as important as any other food culture. Why do we give it so little respect in terms of the Irish food story?

The meaning and value, and thus the taste, of food are always contingent on its circumstances.

Sausages

Unfortunately, there is not much demand for fresh pork meat in Ireland, unless it's transformed into sausages. You'll find pork chops and the occasional pork fillet in the supermarket, but other than that, it all goes into making bacon, ham and sausages. Thankfully, many Irish sausage producers are making excellent sausages and even charcuterie, from Kelly's of Newport to Gubbeen in West Cork.

So what is an Irish sausage? In contrast to British sausages (which are usually made with breadcrumbs), Irish sausages are traditionally made from pork, pork fat, rusk (a form of hardened bread) and seasoning, usually salt, pepper, mace and nutmeg. This penchant for spices in our sausages surely stems from the arrival of the Normans in Ireland, and interestingly, sausage-making goes back to at least the 12th century here. Some sausage-makers forgo rusk and use only meat and fat. I recall making sausages once with butcher Hugh Maguire with only a pork belly going through the grinder.

Nowadays, a myriad of other flavours goes into sausages in Ireland. Spring onion and black pepper are in vogue at the moment. And whatever about the tomato or the hash brown, a full Irish breakfast must include sausages. I say *sausages* because I always expect two. Nothing is worse than a full Irish breakfast with only one sausage.

For most Irish people, the first sausage that springs to mind is the famous Superquinn sausage. Even though the Superquinn chain of supermarkets no longer exists, the sausages are now made by another supermarket chain, SuperValu, and still have a cult following.

These sausages were invented in the north side of Dublin in the early 1980s by Jimmy Canavan and his team of butchers. Feargal Quinn, the founder of the chain of supermarkets, was inspired by German sausages, particularly those from Nuremberg. Speaking about the sausages in 2013, Quinn said, 'We thought of price, health and taste. We said we'll go for taste because nobody who is into healthy eating goes for sausages anyway' (Horgan-Jones 2019).

A simple thing in and of itself, a sausage can tell the story both of Irish food and food in Ireland, from the use of heritage and rare-breed pigs to the spices that evoke flavours from distant lands.

The future of the Irish sausage is in safe hands, especially in the form of pork charcuterie. Ireland has a 30-year-old tradition of producing good-quality charcuterie. Frank Krawczyk established West Cork Salamis in the late 1990s. Fingal Ferguson has been making Gubbeen chorizo and salami in West Cork for 20 years. In Oughterard in Co. Galway, McGeough's Butchers has been making air-dried lamb for at least the same amount of time. Though we may no longer be in the infancy of our charcuterie development on this island, this tradition needs to continue. New charcuterie producers are emerging all the time. In 2016, Dublin butcher Rick Higgins teamed up with Antonio Princigallo to launch a range of Irish artisan charcuterie under the brand Forage & Cure.

Let's hope both of our sausage traditions continue to develop into the future and grow to become part and parcel of the Irish food experience.

There is so much more to Irish food than the potato.

068

Potatoes

It irks me greatly when people associate Ireland purely with the potato. It's a footnote to Irish food, not the main story. It's from Peru, after all. While the spud did sustain us for a few hundred years and contributed to a famine (the blight wasn't the only factor – so was our dependence on it, which wasn't our fault), we lived quite happily on this island for thousands of years without it. There is so much more to Irish food than the potato.

And yet, we love potatoes. We can't seem to have a meal without them. We have as many potato dishes as the Inuit people have words for snow. I jest, of course, but from the moment they arrived in Ireland (and subsequently planted in England), they took off. The Irish have not come first in many things in the world, but we were the first European country to adopt the potato 'as a serious food crop' (Mac Con Iomaire and Óg Gallagher 2009: 167).

Contemporary writers observed how the Irish ate potatoes, usually in a simple manner, by cooking the potato in the embers of the fire and eating it with salt and butter. A book published anonymously in 1732 describes the several ways potatoes are cooked and eaten in Ireland: 'fried, or stewed with onions and salt, with a little ale or small beer and water, or baked with herrings, sweet herbs, pepper and salt, vinegar and water, which dish is not a little admired by those who told me of it' (Anonymous 1732). Other books describe them as being eaten with pork, bacon and salt beef. In his collection of stories from the National Folklore Collection Schools' Collection, John Creedon observes that 'as late as 1939, poorer farming families depended primarily on three staples: milk, potatoes and flour' (Creedon 2022: 122).

Whether you love them or loathe them, you cannot escape the potato when you come to Ireland. However, with each passing generation, and the more global our diet becomes – older generations still regard pasta and rice with some suspicion – the less we focus and therefore depend on the humble spud. However, a newer generation of famers, such as Ballymakenny Farm in Co. Louth, are introducing heritage varieties such as Mayan Gold and Pink Fir Apple to the market.

Boxty

For many, boxty is a symbol of Irishness in terms of potatoes and bread. It appears in many guises. Boxty can be in the form of a bread, a cake, a pancake and even a dumpling. The most common way of making boxty consisted of combining grated raw potato and mashed potato with flour and frying it. Later recipes added bicarbonate of soda to help it rise and buttermilk for moisture. An egg is often added for texture. Nowadays the mixture is fried in a pan, but in the past, it would have been cooked directly on the hotplate of a range.

As with champ and colcannon (see below), there is no set way of making boxty. It depends on the equipment one has – pan boxty, boiled boxty, griddle boxty and loaf boxty are some regional variations. Boxty is associated with many different parts of Ireland, though the North-west seems to lay the strongest claim to it. Longford and Leitrim play a major part in the story of boxty, but many other counties also have a tradition of making it.

An old Irish rhyme that referred to the bread went: 'Boxty on the griddle, boxty on the pan. If you can't make boxty, you'll never get a man.' This seemingly playful rhyme demonstrates the importance of food in relation to marriage and the domestic sphere and what was expected of women in the 19th century.

The origin of the name is unclear, though it may come from the Irish language, possibly from *arán bocht tí*, which means 'poor house bread', or perhaps *bácús*, which means 'bakehouse'.

Champ/cally

Some may argue that the difference between champ and colcannon is purely semantic. Both are made from potatoes and some type of greens. It may come down to whether cabbage is used, but I have found versions that include cabbage. In *Irish Traditional Cooking* (1995:

149), Darina Allen includes some wonderful variations, including Claragh champ (with peas), leek and crispy onion champ (made with beef dripping), nettle champ, leek champ and wild garlic champ.

Cally is a Dublin version of champ made with green onions. Pandy was yet another variation, which was often served to children. It required 'a soft floury spud [...] yellow butter and a drop of milk or spoon of cream skimmed off the top of the bucket, followed by a shake of salt' (Taylor 1994). In some parts of the country, dillisk seaweed (dulse) was often added to mashed potatoes to create a dillisk champ. The dried seaweed would be rehydrated in milk to give a saline flavour to the mash.

Champ, according to Florence Irwin in her book *The Cookin' Woman: Irish Country Recipes* (1949), was traditionally mashed by the 'man of the house' with a 'bettle', a heavy wooden pounder that whipped the potato, milk and vegetables/herbs together.

In Ulster, champ was a favourite Friday night dinner. After being whipped together, it would be served in bowls. A hole would be made it the centre of the mash and a large lump of butter would be placed in it: 'Then the champ would be eaten from the outside with a spoon or fork, dipping it into the melting butter in the centre. All was washed down with new milk or freshly churned buttermilk' (Irwin 1949: 95).

Despite its humble origins, champ is now known the world over, even though it often gets mistaken for a British dish. However, given the shared heritage of our islands, it's often difficult to pinpoint the exact origin of a dish in time and place.

Colcannon

Colcannon is a traditional Irish dish originally made from leftover potatoes combined with cabbage, kale or other greens. The word *colcannon* possibly derives from the Welsh for leek soup, *cawl cennin*, which also contains potatoes. The dish likely originated from combining leftover potatoes with leeks and water to form a new meal.

It receives one of its first modern-day mentions in 1735, when the Welshman William Bulkeley dined on a dish called 'Coel Callen' in Dublin and wrote about it in his diary entry for 31 October:

> Dined at Coz. Wm. Parry [Dublin], and also supped there upon a Shoulder of Mutton rosted, and what they call there Coel Callen which is Cabbage boiled Potatoes & parsnips, all this mixed together, they eat well enough, and it is a Dish always had in this Kingdom on this night. Apples, nuts Ale &c. after Suppe.

Bulkeley's observation suggests that the dish of colcannon was enjoyed frequently at Halloween in Ireland.

There are many variations of colcannon from all over Ireland, with cabbage, spring onions and parsley all playing their part. In *The Cookin' Woman*, Florence Irwin (1949) describes making mashed potatoes with nettles. In coastal areas, seaweed was folded into potatoes.

The dish was the subject of a famous 19th-century folk song:

> *Did you ever eat colcannon when 'twas made with yellow*
> *cream?*
> *And the kale and pratties blended like the picture in a dream?*
> *Did you ever take a forkful, and dip it in the lake*
> *Of the heather-flavoured butter that your mother used to*
> *make?*
> *Oh, you did; yes, you did. So did he and so did I,*
> *And the more I think about it, sure the more I want to cry.*
> *Ah, God be with the happy times, when troubles we had not*
> *And our mothers made colcannon in the little three-legged pot.*

Colcannon is associated with St Brigid and thus the feast day that celebrates her, which takes place on February 1st. It is called *Lá Fhéile Bríde* in Irish and marks the beginning of spring and the Gaelic festival of Imbolc. According to the National Museum of Ireland – Country Life in Castlebar, Co. Mayo, the traditional mealfor families on February 1st was a plate of potatoes and freshly churned butter. St Brigid is the patron saint of dairy farmers, so butter and milk have long been associated with St Brigid's Day. Adding cabbage to the potatoes and butter was also traditional and family members would take turns pounding the potatoes. This simple meal was Ireland's Thanksgiving of sorts: a small feast to give thanks for the previous year's crops as well as hope for the next season's food. Afterwards the family would make their St Brigid's crosses, accompanied by a slice of apple cake or barmbrack, all washed down with a cup of milky tea.

Fisherman's potatoes

Cooking potatoes in the ground is something you might expect from the native peoples of Peru or New Zealand, but it was also a practice among many fishermen in the West of Ireland when they were without a pot for their spuds.

FitzGibbon (1983: 172) writes: 'On the beach dig a pit about 5cm deep. Put the potatoes in their skins into the pit and shovel sand back over them. Light a fire on top. It is said the potatoes will be cooked in a little over half an hour.'

These fisherman's potatoes are a little-known facet of the Irish food story and point to the many more stories that still need to be uncovered.

Potato & onions

This is a long-forgotten 'dish' that used to be served alongside a glass of cool buttermilk after a long day working on the bog. Sliced onions would be fried in bacon dripping, then finely sliced potatoes would be added to the frying pan and all would be cooked down until the potatoes were tender. As with other potato dishes (such as champ and colcannon), there are many seasonal variations, with nettles, wild garlic, dillisk and even raw egg, which was 'a very common dinner for country children' (Irwin 1949: 94).

Potato cakes

There are probably as many recipes for potato cakes as there are words for potato in Irish. Every region and home seems to have subtly different versions with a similar outcome. Making them is not unlike the production of gnocchi, except self-raising flour is used to give the cakes a rise. Interestingly, variations include ones made with caraway seeds and a large one shaped to fit into a flan tin. Indeed, boxty is a type of potato cake save for the fact that it includes raw potato. Yet there are boxty recipes that don't include raw potato.

In their book *Some Experiences of an Irish RM* (1899), Somerville and Ross included the following passage on potato cakes:

> While I live I shall not forget her potato cakes. They came in hot and hot from an oven-pot, they were speckled with caraway seeds, they swam in salt butter, and we ate them shamelessly and greasily, and washed them down with hot whisky and water. I knew to a nicety how ill I should be next day, and I heeded not.

Whiskey and potato cakes does sound like a recipe for indulgence, but it encapsulates an aspect of Irish food and drink culture, even if the RM (resident magistrate) was firmly in the Anglo-Irish sphere.

Potato pie

I cannot imagine eating this 18th-century recipe from the manuscript of Sara Power (1746): a pie made from potatoes, butter, brandy, sugar and eggs, covered with puff pastry, baked for an hour and served hot. One variation includes whiskey and almond flour. I'm not sure if it's a savoury dish or a dessert. With half a pound of sugar and half a pound of butter to a pound of potatoes, I'll leave the decision up to you.

Stampy

Food historian Regina Sexton describes stampy as a 'deluxe version of boxty bread' (1998: 82). Only served on special occasions, perhaps due to the luxurious nature of its ingredients, it included cream, sugar and caraway seeds, among other ingredients. It was generally made to celebrate or commemorate and could be served at the end of the potato harvest, religious events or Halloween.

An entry on stampy bread that was recorded as part of the Schools' Collection from the National Folklore Collection details the making of the bread thus (made much the same way as boxty):

Long ago stampy bread was much used. To make it the man of the house got a piece of tin and holed it with a nail or an awl. This served as a grater. Then the woman got six or seven big raw potatoes and peeled them She grated these on the grater into bowl or basin. Then she put the grated mash into a cloth and squeezed all the moisture out of it into a bowl.

She kept this liquid because she got starch out of it. Then she put the raw potatoes on the bread board and an equal quantity of flour and of boiled mashed potatoes. She mixed them together and wet the mixture with butter milk. She baked it on a griddle till both sides were brown. Then she took it up and buttered it. It had to be eaten hot (Mrs Mac Namara, Loughmore Common, Co. Limerick).

069

Puffin

While writing *The Irish Cookbook* (McMahon 2020), I posted a tweet looking for a puffin to cook. We had eaten puffin on this island, after all, and I wanted to try to be as authentic as possible in my pursuit of Irish food. I wasn't entirely surprised when the Irish Wildlife Trust got back to me and said that they were a protected species. (I was tempted to reply that I only wanted one, but I let it pass.)

Puffins are still eaten in Iceland, but the idea of travelling there to get a puffin and bring it back in my suitcase seemed like a long shot. So instead I talked to my Icelandic chef friend Gunnar Gíslason about it. Gunnar described puffin as a kind of sea pigeon, only 'more beautiful'.

The monks of Skellig ate puffin, mackerel and gull's eggs in the early Middle Ages in Ireland and I'm sure many more coastal communities feasted on them over the millennia that we have occupied this island. While we may not eat puffin anymore, its presence should at least show us that the story of Irish food is often not what we think it is.

On that note, seal would also have often been on the menu, especially for larger banquets. Seal remains from the Middle Ages have been found at many castles around Ireland, including Maynooth Castle outside Dublin. These remains date from the 13th to the 15th centuries.

In his memoir, Joseph C. Walker (1788) observed, 'In one of the largest islands, called Owey, they used to kill a great number of seals which they salted for winter and were so fond of it as to prefer it to any other meat.' Indeed, many islanders off the west coast only ceased eating seal from the 1970s onwards.

Considering a large number of seals are culled each year to control the population, is it time to reintroduce them into the Irish diet? Having tried roasted seal flipper in Canada, I can safely say it tasted good – like a pig that had been swimming in the sea.

The story of Irish food is often not what we think it is.

070

Rabbit

The Irish have mixed feelings about rabbit. When I was growing up, they were a pest for farmers. In 1954, farmers illegally infected the rabbit population with myxomatosis. I will never forget the huge cull of infected rabbits that took place every year. Whenever I thought about rabbits as a boy, I thought about these diseased ones, with their puffy faces and blind eyes.

In the 1950s, Ireland was awash with rabbits, and they were readily available as a cheap source of food. In his book *The Islander* (*An t-Oileánach*), published in 1929, Tomás Ó Crohan (2013) writes of catching 96 rabbits on the Blasket Islands when he was young. Monica Sheridan wrote in her book *The Art of Irish Cooking* (1965), 'Until about ten years ago, Ireland was overrun with wild rabbits. They became a positive plague in the country, eating the vegetables in the garden and the crops in the fields. At one time they could be bought in the city shops for twelve cents apiece, while in the country they cost no more than the price of a shotgun cartridge.'

By the 1960s, this had all changed. Disease was widespread and the consumption of rabbits effectively ceased. Because myxomatosis made rabbits look horrid, it turned everyone off them, even if they were healthy. In 1985, there was a veritable plague of rabbits on the largest of the Aran Islands. RTÉ footage from the time shows people struggling to keep the rabbit population under control, as the rabbits were eating all the grass that was supposed to be for the cows.

Nowadays, people seem to want to have them as pets, not eat them. We still get a delivery of wild rabbit once a week in Aniar. I combine rabbit with nettles in spring and wild mushrooms in autumn.

In terms of its history in Ireland, rabbit was popular as a food and for its fur. Following on from the Romans (and their penchant for rabbits), the Normans introduced rabbits to Ireland in the late 12th century. Rabbit meat (especially that of newborn rabbits) seems to have been a food that was allowed during Lent in the Early Christian period. Rabbit bones were found at many medieval sites, from castles (Trim Castle, Co. Meath) to abbeys (Tintern Abbey, Co. Wexford), thus demonstrating their popularity as a food source.

Because of the British desire for rabbit fur, rabbits became a major export from Ireland in the 17th century. Of course, their meat was also exported to England and eaten in large quantities, although initially rabbit meat was the preserve of the rich. There are several recipes for rabbit stew from this period in English cookbooks, so we can assume that similar dishes were made in Ireland too. Rabbit pie was also popular – recipes for it featured in older Irish cookbooks of the early to mid-20th century. Bacon was generally included, as rabbit meat is very lean.

With the rise of cheap chicken, the popularity of rabbit waned in the latter half of the 20th century. As with all wild food, people rejected it following their increased wealth, though some still cooked it – in *The Cookin' Woman*, Florence Irwin (1949) includes a recipe for curried rabbit and rice. However, by the time I was a boy, everyone had turned to chicken. This is unfortunate, as wild rabbit is a much more ethical and sustainable choice than battery chicken. Eating it also connects you with a 1,000-year-long tradition of its consumption on the island of Ireland. Though once referred to as 'poor man's chicken', rabbit is a valuable food, with its own unique, gamey flavour. I hope the popularity of its consumption returns. Chef Paul Flynn's rabbit tureen is a beautiful dish that encapsulates the continuation of the tradition of eating rabbit in Ireland.

o 7 1

Rapeseed

Cold-pressed rapeseed oil is Ireland's answer to extra-virgin olive oil. Some may disagree, saying that rapeseed oil is too floral and too heavy, but if we are to learn what our own food tastes like, then we need to use the food that surrounds us. I'm not saying olive oil (or any other oil) is inferior; it's just different. At Aniar, we always fry, dress and finish dishes with rapeseed oil. It gives our food a flavour of the Irish landscape.

During the late spring and early summer months, yellow fields of rapeseed flowers can be seen up and down the country, especially in the east, from Louth down to Kilkenny. Newgrange Gold Rapeseed Oil, which is farmed, pressed and bottled in the Boyne Valley in Co. Meath, is just one of the many cold-pressed rapeseed oils being produced in Ireland now. Donegal Rapeseed Oil is another brand that produces oil from rapeseed grown by Donegal farmers that was previously exported to England for processing.

As with our native sea salt industry, our indigenous oil industry is still small. As the culture of Irish food grows, hopefully this essential food product will too. If we want our food to taste like the place where it is cooked, then using cold-pressed rapeseed oil to fry and dress our food can help us achieve this. A few drops over charred Irish asparagus can evoke the aromas of sunny May days in Ireland when the yellow rapeseed flowers can be seen in the fields.

If we are to learn what our food tastes like, then we need to use the food that surrounds us.

072

Rhubarb

Rhubarb demonstrates the truly global power of food over many thousands of years. However, it may surprise you to know that for most of its existence, rhubarb was used as a medicine rather than a food. The Greeks and Romans used the roots to alleviate (or at least try to alleviate) many ailments, including constipation. It is only in the past 200 years that rhubarb has emerged as a culinary ingredient in Ireland and elsewhere for desserts and wine.

Indeed, a rhubarb craze occurred in the 19th century due to the accidental discovery of how to grow forced rhubarb. Yorkshire, with its Rhubarb Triangle, subsequently came to dominate production. In the early 20th century, 90% of the world's forced winter rhubarb came from there.

Forced rhubarb is produced by growing the vegetable outside for two years. The exposure to frost toughens the roots before the plant is moved into dark 'forcing sheds'. Once in these sheds, heat is applied, which causes the stalks to grow quickly in search of light. This quick growth produces a rhubarb that is soft, sweet and tart all at once, with delicately vivid red and white colours. Forced rhubarb cooks extremely quickly. In fact, it is so tender it can be eaten raw. Many older Irish people remember it being dipped in sugar and served as a sweet treat or used in rhubarb tarts in the darker days of January and February.

073

Ribena

Ribena is a drink that breaks down the thorny divisions between Ireland and England. Though essentially a British drink, blackcurrants for Ribena were grown on the Jeffares farm in Co. Wexford from 1955 to 2013.

At the outset Ribena was associated with health, especially vitamin C. It was developed in the late 1930s by Dr Vernon Charley, a scientist at the University of Bristol. It became important for the war effort when oranges were in short supply.

Though over the years both the fruit and the sugar content of Ribena have been brought into question (as well as the amount of vitamin C it contained), the drink has always retained a warm affinity in the Irish consciousness. Nowadays, though, Ribena seems to have lost its hold on the Irish imagination and Jeffares now make their own blackcurrant cordial, which is available in most Irish supermarkets.

°74

Rice

Rice became more common in Ireland after the failure of the potato during the Irish Famine. It was often added to soups and broths, such as mutton broth, and used interchangeably with pearl barley. However, it would be wrong to think that rice has not played a part in the Irish diet for the last couple of hundred years. Though not as notable as the potato (which is also an immigrant; see page 123), rice has maintained an ambiguous relationship to Ireland, with an indelible association with foreignness or otherness.

Florence Irwin includes a curried rabbit and rice recipe in *The Cookin' Woman: Irish Country Recipes* (1949). Though you may find the inclusion of curry or rice in a mid-20th-century Irish cookbook strange, Irwin was a great traveller and looked on cooking with the eye of an anthropologist. If curried rabbit and rice was being cooked in Ireland, then she included it in her book. I didn't see a rabbit until I opened my own restaurant in 2008, let alone a curried rabbit. But such is the way traditions rise and fall over the years.

Rice pudding

For my grandmother's generation, rice was for dessert. Pudding rice is a specific type of short-grain rice (like Arborio) that is used for making sweet rice pudding, especially in Ireland and the UK.

Rice pudding dates to the Tudor period in England and probably made its way across to Ireland in the 17th century. Recipe books from the period, such as *The English Huswife* by Gervase Markham (1615), refer to rice pudding as 'whitepot' due to the colour of the pot when the cream went in:

> Take the best and sweetest cream, and boil it with good store of sugar, and cinnamon, and a little rose-water, then take it from the fire and put into it clean picked rice, but not so

much as to make it thick, and let it steep therein till it be cold; then put in the yolks of six eggs, and two whites, currants, sugar, cinnamon, and rose-water, and salt, then put it into a pan, or pot, as thin as if it were a custard; and so bake it and serve it in the pot it is baked in, trimming the top with a little sugar or comfits.

Though my great-grandmother may not have realised it, each time she was making rice pudding with cinnamon, sugar, nutmeg or jam, she was continuing a tradition that dated back over 400 years.

Rice pudding is rarely made in Irish homes nowadays, but I see plenty of pudding rice as well as ready-made rice puddings on the shelves of the supermarket, so someone must be eating it.

Monica Sheridan's shellfish soup in *The Art of Irish Cooking* (1965) contains saffron and seaweed, which represent the two sides of Irish cooking: one that looks out to the world and the other that focuses on the land at home.

075

Saffron

When it first arrived in Ireland, saffron was used as a dye for tweed and other fabrics. Saffron was used as a dye by the Celts of Northern Europe from at least as far back as the time of Christ.

The great Irish mantle was a type of loose, knee-length tunic (*léine croich*) that was normally saffron-coloured. Edmund Spenser, a 16th-century English writer and poet, describes the great Irish mantle as 'their house, their tent, their couch, their target [shield]' (1897). From about the 17th century, the gentry in Ireland stopped wearing tunics and started imitating English dress, except in the West and Northwest. However, there was a revival in the 18th century, which kept the wearing of the saffron mantle alive.

From the 18th century onwards, saffron was used in breads, cakes and even soup. James Joyce's *Ulysses* (1922) includes a mention of saffron buns. In her book *In An Irish Country Kitchen*, Clare Connery (1993) observes that saffron was used to colour mussel soup in the past, while Monica Sheridan's shellfish soup in *The Art of Irish Cooking* (1965) contains saffron and seaweed, which represent the two sides of Irish cooking: one that looks out to the world and the other that focuses on the land at home.

According to Theodora FitzGibbon (1983), saffron cake most likely originates from Cornwall. Bríd Mahon writes that saffron cakes were eaten on Good Friday and were also given to children 'suffering from the measles' (1991: 76). The recipe for saffron cake included in FitzGibbon's *Irish Traditional Food* (1983) comes from the handwritten manuscript of Sara Power and dates to 1746. Barm (*see also* 'Barmbrack', page 14) is used as the leavening agent for the cake. Power observes that your 'barm must settle for 40 hours before you can use it' and 'your oven must not be too hot' lest your cake dry out. Wise words indeed.

076
Salt

It's hard to think about cooking without salt, but the first Mesolithic migrants who came to Ireland did not use salt for the first few thousand years. It was only after the Agricultural Revolution in the mid-17th century that people needed additional salt in their diet.

The first salt was most likely produced only in coastal regions by trapping water in 'pans' and allowing it to evaporate. The Celts were experts in mining salt in Central Europe, so we can only assume that they brought their technology of salt production with them to Ireland. The Celts knew the value of salt – the word *salary* derives from the word *salt* in Latin, which was used in Ireland to pay for many things, including as tributes or votive offerings. The 8th-century text *Conall Corc and the Corco Luigde* records that the Aran Islanders paid a tribute of salt to the King of Cashel.

Another method of possible salt production in Ireland is detailed in Nikolah Gilligan's essay 'Salt from Seaweed? An Experimental Archaeology Perspective on Salt in Early Medieval Ireland' (2020). A type of black salt can be produced by burning seaweed and boiling it with seawater, then evaporating the water. The resulting ash can then be used to season and cure foodstuffs. Gilligan did tests and concluded, 'It is therefore proposed that some of the salt in early medieval Ireland was produced from seaweed, by drying it, burning it, soaking the ashes in water, removing the charcoal and boiling or allowing the water to evaporate until salt is produced.' Her tests are corroborated historically by other accounts of the production of black salt by the Scottish people of the Western Isles, as detailed in M. Martin's *A Description of the Western Islands of Scotland* (1703). Martin includes references to 'the ashes of burnt sea-ware' (seaweed) used to cure meat and fish in the Scottish Western Isles at the close of the 17th century.

In the Middle Ages, English salt was imported into Ireland by the Anglo-Norman elites. English salt was seen (and still is, to a certain degree – think of Maldon or Halen Môn) as a superior salt. Though it's unclear whether the Celts mined Ireland for salt, modern salt mines do exist, but nowadays they mostly produce salt for gritting roads. Up until the end of the 19th century, most Irish ports had facilities to produce salt, but this practice died out over time due to cheaper imports becoming available.

It is only in the last few years that Ireland has started to produce excellent sea salt to rival its English and French counterparts. My favourite is a sea salt produced on Achill Island by the Achill Island Sea Salt Company. Their flaky crystals are some of the finest in the world. We use it to finish all our dishes in Aniar.

There are other Irish salt companies, such as Oriel Sea Salt in Co. Louth, Dingle Sea Salt, Irish Atlantic Sea Salt and West of Dingle Sea Salt. I hope this new small-scale salt production blooms into a world-renowned industry. We have some of the finest salt in the world in Ireland, yet we fail to recognise its inherent value in its ability to give our food a unique flavour.

°77

Scones

There is a long tradition of baking scones in Ireland. Before ovens, they were made on griddle pans or with the aid of a cast iron bakestone that could be placed directly in the fire.

The origin of the scone dates to 1513 in print, but small cakes made from oats are certainly older. Before the advent of refined flours, scones were made with oats and a variety of different flours. There are many types of scones in Ireland, from drop scones, treacle scones, ones laced with honey and ones made with Indian meal (maize) to seeded ones (caraway) and ones made with potato and oatmeal. A little like the number of our potato dishes, the Irish seem to have been incredibly inventive when it comes to turning a simple scone into a multitude of variations according to the availability of ingredients.

In his autobiography, Irish playwright Seán O'Casey fondly recalls having homemade scones and tea in Dublin with his mother, scones that were 'well warmed in the oven, melting in your mouth before you'd time to sink your teeth in them (O'Casey 1980a: 14).

My mother never stopped making scones. Plain ones, brown ones, fruit ones. During my teenage years, my friends were afraid to call to the house because she would keep insisting that they have a scone – a real-life Mrs Doyle but with scones instead of tea. Baking scones was a true sign of Irish hospitality that continues to this day and demonstrates the generosity embedded inside the Irish food story.

Baking scones was a true sign of Irish hospitality that continues to this day and demonstrates the generosity embedded inside the Irish food story.

078

Sea herbs

It feels wrong to lump all the herbs that grow by the sea into one section, as there are dozens of them. Sea herbs such as samphire, sea beet and sea radish are some of the earliest foodstuffs eaten in Ireland. Hunter-gatherers would have certainly consumed them. They would have played an important part in the diet in terms of vitamins and minerals. They are also some of the most plentiful yet underused of our indigenous foodstuffs, to the point that they have almost been forgotten.

Looking through the Irish recipe books of the past century, you would think we had no tradition of using these wild herbs. Apart from sea beet being used in soup or samphire cooked in butter, it's hard to find other recipes. I don't know if this is because cookbooks excluded them due to their limited availability (they have to be foraged) or because they weren't part of a specific written tradition. As with seaweed, just because we have no written record of sea herbs, it doesn't mean they played no part in our food culture in the past.

Sea beet, orache, arrowgrass, samphire, sea purslane, sea kale, sea radish: these words were once a foreign language to me. Little did I know that they (along with seaweed) would become a staple part of our larder in Aniar. I can't imagine cooking without them. These wondrous indigenous plants not only represent a connection with our past on this island, they also represent our future and the possibilities we may create for them in the context of Irish food. They are as vital now for the Irish food story as they were 10,000 years ago for the first settlers on this island.

°79
Seafood, river fish & shellfish

Fish and shellfish have been an important resource in Ireland since the arrival of the first settlers. The first settlements were all based near water (mostly the sea), with occasional inland settlements beside rivers and lakes. Water was the lifeblood of the first communities until farming arrived a couple of thousand years later.

To say the Irish have a strained relationship with seafood is an understatement. There are many possible reasons for this phenomenon, from famine and fasting to colonialism and a predilection towards farming. From the Neolithic period onwards, fish fell away as an absolute necessity as people turned towards animals such as cattle, pigs, sheep and goats (Mallory 2015: 74). Is this one reason why the modern Irish rejected fish for so long? Could a change that happened thousands of years ago still affect so many of us now?

As a family, we never ate shellfish. My aunt, now in her mid-seventies, has told me that she has never eaten fish and never will. The closest I got to fresh fish when I was growing up were bony whiting fillets that were lightly floured and pan-fried. I used to tremble eating them, as I was scared half to death from being told to be careful not to choke on the bones.

I think many of us were scared of fish. Is it any surprise we turned against fish and retreated to the land of beef, chicken and pork? Why would I want to eat something that might kill me? Donegal Catch or fish fingers were a safer bet. I had to travel to Spain to first eat (or rather, enjoy eating) Irish fish, which sums up our miserable and contested relationship with the ocean.

This is not to say that this is the case for everyone on the island, but it does mirror the experience of many people I have spoken to over the years. When did we turn away from the ocean? Was it during the first Agricultural Revolution? Was it due to colonialism and a lack of opportunity to get out to sea? It was probably a little bit of both. Yet for most of the time on the island of Ireland, fish was abundant and essential. Monks had well-stocked lakes near their abbeys, which led in turn to the importance of fisheries in early and medieval Ireland as a food source. In his influential account of Ireland from 1188, *Topographia Hiberniae* (*Topography of Ireland*), Gerald of Wales mentions Ireland's lakes 'abounding in fish':

> The rivers and lakes also are plentifully stored with the sorts of fish peculiar to these waters especially four species, salmon, trout, muddy eels and oily shad. The Shannon abounds in lamprey, a dangerous delicacy indulged in by the wealthy. This country, however, does not produce some fine fishes found in other countries, and some excellent fresh-water fishes, such as the pike, the perch, the roach, the barbel, the gardon (Giraldus Cambrensis 2000: 15).

Later accounts, such as Arthur Young's *A Tour in Ireland* (1887), detail 'five hundred children fishing at the same time', catching everything from large pike to bream, tench and trout as well as salmon.

We are in a much better position in the 21st century to love and appreciate fish, though many of our fishermen still struggle due to EU quotas and we export the vast majority of that catch. It seems we gave away our rights to our fishing grounds in order to export beef to the EU and further afield unimpeded. This practice is tied to the legacy of the British use of Ireland as a grazing ground for cattle as well as the focus on cattle as a commodity in ancient Ireland (*see also* 'Beef', page 16). As this section attests, we have an amazing number of fish and shellfish in Irish waters. We need to embrace them more if we want them to continue to be part of our food story.

Ballan wrasse

Wrasse was once an important fish for the people of the Aran Islands, who would salt and dry it to preserve it for the winter. Salted wrasse with white sauce was once a typical Christmas Eve dish on the Aran Islands.

Of the five wrasse species, Ballan wrasse (*Labrus bergylta*) is the largest and swims among the rocks close to shore, feeding off mussels and limpets. The fish was more widely available in the past, but you rarely see it these days, as it is often used as bait for more expensive things such as lobster. As Máirtín Mac Con Iomaire (2005: 29) observes in his essay 'The History of Seafood in Irish Cuisine and Culture', 'its popularity has been waning over the last two decades'.

In 14 years of running Aniar, I have come across salted wrasse twice. Perhaps it is a tradition that some food entrepreneur should reignite, especially given the international fame of salted cod (*bacalao*) in the Basque region.

Chowder

To this day, many Americans coming to Ireland go in search of a big bowl of chowder, buttered wedges of brown soda bread, a pint of Guinness and a roaring fire (even in July). But how Irish is chowder, actually?

I'm not saying that we don't make it. I used to love making the chowder when I worked as a young chef in Fat Freddy's in Galway in the late nineties and early aughts. Back then, not many people were talking about provenance; even fewer were talking about food history. This is not to say no one was. The vanguard was quietly working away on the Irish food story. Maura Laverty's cookbook *Full and Plenty* (1960) includes a cod chowder.

Chowder began its life as a foodstuff to feed English and French sailors as they crossed the Atlantic to Canada and America. In the absence of flour, the soup was thickened with sea biscuits, or what they called 'sailors' crackers'. In his memoirs (Crow 1830), Captain Hugh Crow recalled eating a dish called chowder that consisted of 'a mixture of fresh fish, salt pork, pounded biscuit and onions; and which, when well-seasoned and stewed, we found to be an excellent palatable dish'.

From its inauspicious origins for sailors and seamen to its central place in the culinary psychology of many New Englanders, chowder now occupies a strange place in Irish food culture. Perhaps as opposed to being only Irish, it's a dish that forms a bridge that allows us to connect to our overseas cousins in England and America.

Cockles

Archaeological evidence shows that cockles, as well as other shellfish such as scallops and limpets, were an important foodstuff for the first peoples here. Cockles were once a popular street food in coastal towns, simply boiled and seasoned with vinegar, salt and pepper. Cockles were also pickled and sold in jars, though this practice has all but ceased with modern methods of preservation. The practice of pickling shellfish probably dates to at least the Viking settlements.

Though not made much these days, cockle soup was popular in coastal areas in the past, particularly in the West of Ireland. When flour was unavailable to thicken the soup, oatmeal would be used. The resulting soup would have a 'lovely nutty flavour' (FitzGibbon 1983: 20).

Monica Sheridan's shellfish soup in *The Art of Irish Cooking* (1965) contains cockles as well as saffron and seaweed – an interesting combination from a foodways point of view, as it challenges our ideas of what Irish food was in the 1950s.

Cockles were often eaten with laverbread (an oat bread made with nori seaweed) and bacon in Sligo, though this tradition is more famously associated with Wales. Cockles abound on the sandy beaches of Connemara. In Kerry, they are called carpetshell and kirkeen.

The simplest way to cook them is to add them to boiling seawater until they open, then scoop them out and add some butter. Sinead O'Donnell-Carey remembers, 'While at my Granny's in Donegal, we would often go out and pick cockles, then fry them in real butter and put them on a slice of her scone of bread.'

Crab

To tell the story of the Irish brown crab, we must go back at least 9,000 years to the summer settlements of the first hunter-gatherers who made coastal areas their home. Without recourse to pots (which would not come along for another couple of thousand years), the crabs would undoubtedly have been cooked over an open fire, then cracked open with rocks.

Crab served on soda bread as an open sandwich may be Ireland's answer to the Danish *smørrebrød*. We should market it better, as it is a truly wonderful sandwich. Crab claws in garlic butter is a common sight on pub menus all over Ireland, especially near coastal towns. Potted crab will sometimes appear on menus, though it bears little relationship to true potted crab. Potting was a method of preservation (for prawns, herring, trout and beef, among other foods) that covered the food item in butter to keep it from spoiling so that it could be used in the future, especially in the winter months. Nowadays, it mostly just means picked crab in a Kilner jar. This is not to cast aspersions on its quality – any pub that serves freshly picked crab meat is doing wonders, in my opinion.

Dublin Bay prawns

According to Theodora FitzGibbon, langoustines arrived in Dublin from Norwegian boats that moored in Dublin Bay, hence their name. A Dublin Bay prawn is actually a little lobster, which is why they are also called langoustines and Norwegian lobsters.

Dublin Bay prawns have a long history in Ireland, particularly in Dublin, where they were hawked by fishmongers in the streets. There are many stories of fisherwomen in the early 19th century who cooked and sold langoustines on the streets of the capital. It is said that the fisherwomen would buy stout and linen with the money they made from selling them.

Scampi (which is the Italian name for langoustines) was, and still is, a popular dish in Ireland, though nowadays it's more likely to be made with prawns from South-East Asia. To make scampi, langoustines need to be peeled, then dipped in a light batter and deep-fried. It was a popular starter in Dublin restaurants from the 1950s to the 1990s and you'll still find it on menus around the country.

These days, our Dublin Bay prawns come from Connemara or about 300km west of the Aran Islands. I still welcome the season each year in the West of Ireland, even though more and more of our best langoustines (in terms of size) are being exported, which is a shame. Maybe someday we'll appreciate the best of what we have and keep more of it for ourselves.

Eel

The light glimmers off the waters of Lough Neagh as the eels swim majestically underneath. It is a truly magical place, with thousands of years of food heritage in the form of fishing for, smoking and eating eel. The poet Seamus Heaney, who grew up near Lough Neagh, wrote about these eels in poems such as 'A Lough Neagh Sequence' and 'Eelworks'.

Eel is the apotheosis of Irish food: a symbol of our ancient heritage. Archaeologists have found evidence of eel fishing dating to the Bronze Age. In ancient times, the most efficient way of fishing for eel would have used stationary wooden fish traps at the mouth of freshwater streams during the eels' migration to the sea. There is still evidence of these traps in Dublin. Eel could also be caught using a three-pronged spear. Eel was a source of protein for the poor in the Middle Ages and weirs were established at many locations to catch eel, as well as salmon, along the Shannon, such as the 700-year-old weir in Fergus Estuary in Co. Clare (Went 1950).

Lough Neagh in Northern Ireland is the home of the largest wild-caught eel fishery in Europe. Eel fishing has been a major industry on the lough for centuries. Since 1960, Lough Neagh Fishermen's Co-operative has had the rights to manage the fishery. It now manages the production of around 400 tonnes of eels annually and exports internationally. The eels are brined and then smoked traditionally.

In 2011, Lough Neagh eel was awarded EU Protected Geographical Indication (PGI) status. This European scheme promotes and protects the names of quality agricultural products and foodstuffs that are 'essentially attributable to that place of origin'. Lough Neagh eel is one of the few PGI products in Ireland, along with Clare Island salmon, Connemara Hill lamb, Oriel sea salt and the Waterford blaa, among others.

It's unfortunate that most people don't want to engage with eel nowadays. No doubt this is due to the poor treatment eels received in the past, rendering them overcooked and tasteless. Boiled eel in a heavy white sauce does not sound very appetising. Eel was also associated with poverty, as was most fish.

It's time we re-evaluate our attitude to eel. Though eel stocks are low and most commercial fishing is not allowed, this is no reason not to try it. Smoked eel is a real delicacy – its taste is tied to Irish history. Birgitta Curtin of Burren Smokehouse smokes Lough Neagh eel on the bone in her smokery in Co. Clare.

Fish pie

Fish pies appear often in our shared food history with Britain, if only in the Big Houses of the Anglo-Irish seeking to emulate their British counterparts. They don't seem to be as fashionable as they once were and have largely been consigned to the status of a ready meal now.

The British tradition of fish pie goes all the way back to the time of Henry I, who was crowned in 1100. Henry's cooks rolled crust over an annual Christmas lamprey pie. Lampreys are like eels and were popular to eat in the Middle Ages. They are mentioned by Gerald of Wales as being of good stock in Ireland (Giraldus Cambrensis 2000). Often, the lamprey were bled and the blood was used in the sauce. Though it may seem a tad revolting to be drinking fish blood, it's no different to using pigs' blood to make black pudding.

The tradition of the 'royal fish pie' continued down through the ages. Another tradition required cooks to send the king two dozen pies containing 100 herrings. In Cornwall, a tradition of sticking the heads of pilchards out of a baked pie, called a stargazy pie, continues to this day.

Herring

In the old days, herring was cooked over a turf fire in the Claddagh, the fishing village just outside Galway city (it's now part of the city). Herring was also potted to preserve it for the winter. A recipe for potted herring from 1890 includes bay leaves and pickling spices.

Herring was a vital part of the fish economy in Ireland for hundreds of years. Salted herring in barrels were shipped all over the world from Ireland. A poem written in 1846 by Alfred Perceval Graves (the Bishop of Limerick) declared herring the king of fish in Ireland, over salmon, turbot, cod and ling. No doubt it was the importance of herring to the economy that made this the case. In the 18th century, the English agronomist Arthur Young observed that 'the food of the poor is potatoes, milk and herring' (Young 1887).

Herring is little seen nowadays, which is a shame. The late Gerry Galvin, one of the first chefs in Ireland to focus on Irish food in the 1970s, featured potted herring (accompanied by a salad with spicy tomato dressing) on his menu in Drimcong House (1983–99) in Moycullen (Andrews 2009: 74).

Limpets

Traditionally, limpets were a food for the poor. They were hacked off the rocks with a special chisel and cooked in water or used to form the base of a broth or soup. In his book *The Islander* (*An t-Oileánach*), Tomás Ó Crohan, one of the last residents of the Blasket Islands, writes of his mother bringing a dish of roasted limpets from the strand and 'throwing them to us one by one, like [a] hen with chickens' (2013: 16).

Darina Allen includes a recipe for limpet soup from Co. Kerry in her book *Irish Traditional Cooking* (1995). In his book *The Edible Mollusca of Great Britain and Ireland* (1867), M.S. Lovell also provides a recipe for limpet soup. Interestingly, Lovell says to remove the seaweed attached to the limpets, while Darina Allen reports that the people of Cape Clear would leave the seaweed attached.

Limpets may have also been boiled in seawater and eaten straight up, as they are in other European countries. I've tried to use them in Aniar, but I just couldn't make them edible enough to be pleasurable. In the West of Ireland, many fishermen still refer to them as 'Famine food.'

Lobster

It's hard to imagine that lobsters were once so plentiful that they were used as fertilizer and seen as a kind of 'rat of the sea.'

Lobster abounds on coastal menus around the country, but truth be told, it's probably mostly for tourists. It's expensive because they are caught in small amounts in little pods. The only place I love to eat lobster is in my own home. I don't want to spend good money on an overcooked lobster and chips in a pub.

Once, while cooking lobster on the Aran Islands, a fourth-generation lobster fisherman said to me, 'Have you a burger? I fucking hate lobster!' Our old disdain for seafood comes to the fore in an instant

We never seem to appreciate the food we have in front of us, always in search of something else to satiate our appetite. This is the Irish food story.

in this anecdote. We never seem to appreciate the food we have in front of us, always in search of something else to satiate our appetite. This is the Irish food story.

There was a time when lobster was as cheap as chips (pardon the pun). In her book *Irish Holiday* (1939), social historian Dorothy Hartley, recalling Ireland of the 1920s and the 1930s, writes, 'years ago when I first visited the west [of Ireland], large lobsters averaged 9d [ninepence] each and bread and butter, lobsters and tea were the staple diet' of the people.

In his 1788 account of the people of Rosses Island off Co. Donegal, a clergyman observed:

> Their shellfish they got in the following manner; the men went to rocks with a hook tied to the end of a strong rod; and with that they pulled from under the rocks, as many crabs and lobsters as they wanted; the lobsters commonly weighing from five to twelve pounds each. For scallops and oysters, when the tide was out, the young women waded into the sea where they knew the beds of such fish lay; some of them, naked; others having stripped off their petticoats, went in with their gowns tucked up about their waist; and by armful brought to shore, whatever number of scallops and oysters they though requisite; the scallops weighing from two to four pounds each (Chadbourne 2012: 74).

Perhaps it was a feast of riches that ruined us in the end. Having too much of something, or no alternative, may have pushed us away from the bounties of the sea.

Pickled lobster was common in the 18th century in Ireland, mainly as a way of keeping it fresh (pickling in general was used a lot). Sara Power's manuscript of 1746 includes a recipe for pickled lobster that includes 'little cucumbers', 'musharooms' and a 'branch of rosemary'.

Jammet's, a renowned French restaurant that operated in Dublin between 1901 and 1967, was known for their lobster sauce, which was served with turbot. Jammet's was probably the most famous restaurant in Ireland in the early part of the 20th century. In 1928, *Vogue* described Jammet's as 'one of Europe's best restaurants [...] crowded with gourmets and wits' (F. McDonald 2014). Jammet's is mentioned several times in Irish literature, including in Oliver St John Gogarty's *As I Was Going Down Sackville Street* (1937) and, more famously, in James Joyce's *Ulysses* (1922). Lobsters aside, Jammet's was important for the development of food culture in Dublin, even though it left us in thrall to French cuisine (which is still the case with many of our fine dining restaurants).

Monkfish

There are a number of fish with ugly heads, but monkfish probably pips John Dory to the post. In the 19th century, fishermen were afraid to land monkfish because they thought it was the devil. Its name in German, *Seeteufel*, even translates as 'devil fish'.

Nowadays, though, Irish people enjoy monkfish and it's incredibly popular here. I'm told it's because it feels like you're eating a steak. We have difficulty accepting fish as fish. We like fish that are meaty, not fishy. Along with sea bass, monkfish was one of those fish that everyone had to have during the Celtic Tiger years due to its luxury.

Yet not all countries like monkfish as much as we do. I cooked in Toronto a number of years ago and requested monkfish for the occasion. I wanted to wrap it in kelp and steam it to showcase contemporary Irish food. The chefs asked me why I was cooking with such a contemptible fish. The only place they could source it was Chinatown.

Saying that, monkfish is important in the Irish food story. Monkfish cooked with wild mushrooms, brandy and cream is one way that I cook it to showcase not only the fish but also some other wonderful Irish ingredients. You'll also find a version of scampi made with monkfish tail on menus around the country (Andrews: 2009).

Oysters

'He was a bold man that first ate an oyster,' wrote Jonathan Swift, the celebrated author of *Gulliver's Travels*.

At Mesolithic sites such as Ferriter's Cove (Co. Kerry), Kilnatierny (Co. Down) and Rockmarshall (Co. Louth), archaeologists have uncovered abundant evidence of oyster consumption in midden beds (ancient food dumping grounds consisting of shells and bones). Empty shells of *Ostrea edulis* (the European flat oyster) reside here, buried in the soil. Oysters and other shellfish such as mussels, cockles, limpets, scallops and razor clams would have provided sustenance in the autumn and winter months, when food was less abundant.

The European flat oyster (what we call the 'native' oyster in Ireland) is celebrated every year in September at the Galway International Oyster Festival, which is one of the longest-running food festivals in the world. However, due to disease, pollution and over-harvesting, the Pacific oyster was introduced into Ireland from the 1960s onwards. If you eat oysters in Ireland, this will be the one that you most likely find in restaurants and oysters bar around the country.

Oysters were once associated with the working class and poor. However, the Industrial Revolution dramatically reduced the world's supply of oysters due to the excessive pollution of bays, thus turning them into a luxury item. In the era of the Big House in Ireland (from the 17th to the early 20th century), oysters abounded on menus and are included in the many recipe books from that time. From oyster omelettes and oyster pies to oyster sauces (for game birds) and oysters in collared eels, it seems the Anglo-Irish people of that period couldn't get enough of them.

Perhaps the greatest difficulty in getting Irish people to eat oysters (there are still many people on this island who have never eaten one) is the fact that they are most commonly eaten live and raw. There are few, if any, foodstuffs that we still eat live. This is often an impediment to those who want to try an oyster for the first time.

The combination of oysters and stout (usually Guinness) possibly emerged in the mid-19th century, but its origins are obscure. One of the earliest recorded mentions of Guinness and oysters was by British Prime Minister Benjamin Disraeli, who had them one night in November 1837 and described it as 'the most remarkable day hitherto of my life' (Yenne 2007: 33). Guinness did much to promote the pairing over the course of the 20th century. A 1995 poster for a pub selling bottled Guinness advertised three free oysters with each bottle purchased (Medcalf 2016). The British celebrity chef Marco Pierre White once pontificated about the 'romance' of the combination, eating 'half a dozen oysters' with a half a pint of Guinness in a silver goblet (Sibley 2008). A glorious ritual indeed.

Travelling around Ireland, you will see plenty of oysters paired with Guinness and other stouts, from Keogh's limited-edition Guinness and oyster crisps to beef, stout and oyster pies, and oysters with stout granita. In Aniar, we made our own tribute to this pairing with a stout and nori seaweed sauce that produced the most beautifully contrasting black-and-white dish.

For all their association with the malty quality of stout, I prefer my oysters with something a little more innovative. We often forget that they don't have to only be washed down with stout, lemon or Tabasco (nothing is lazier in the eyes of the expert oyster eater). The next time you have oysters, try them with a dash of buttermilk and wild garlic oil, or with a few strands of pepper dulse, or (my favourite) with some sea lettuce, Goatsbridge trout caviar and Newgrange Gold cold-pressed rapeseed oil from the Boyne Valley.

Periwinkles

Periwinkles are a Mesolithic Irish food. Traditionally, fishermen cooked them on the trawler and ate them with a pin. In Cork, they were served with a pint (and a pin) as a bar snack with lashings of malt vinegar and salt. They can also be blanched and shelled, then deep-fried in batter.

Sadly, most of today's stock of periwinkles are shipped to Spain. Like limpets (see page 154), periwinkles are seldom eaten nowadays in Ireland, though they are a little more pleasurable than limpets.

Pike

The only fish that we ever fished for growing up were pike and perch – but we never dreamed of eating them. We were constantly told they were dirty fish. They lived in the canal, after all. But there was, and still is in some parts of Ireland, a time when many of us ate pike.

Pike in my imagination were the Irish answer to the Amazon piranha. Our primary teacher told us a pack of pike could easily eat the leg off a horse. Walking home from school, I was afraid to put my foot in the canal lest a pike eat it off. Each year, the Maynooth Summer Project would have a competition for fishing on the canal. A pike was always the winning fish. Once I actually managed to catch a pike, but I couldn't land it. It eventually ate through my line and swam off.

When writing *The Irish Cookbook* (McMahon 2020), I went in search of a pike to cook only to be contacted by the Fisheries Board, who told me they were endangered. Endangered by whom, I thought. Weren't they eating all the trout? The late Gerry Galvin famously served pike with bacon and lovage in Drimcong House in Co. Galway. Many older Irish recipes serve pike with bacon, as the fat lent the fish more flavour.

Over time, we have abandoned our rivers as a source of food. Though trout and salmon are still caught (mostly by anglers for sport), other river fish such as carp and tench are no longer on the menu. It would be good to see some of these fish, including pike, find their way back into the Irish food story.

Pollan

Pollan, rarely eaten in Ireland nowadays, is found in only five lakes in Ireland: Lough Neagh, Lower Lough Erne, Lough Ree, Lough Derg and Lough Allen. Though a descendant of an Alaskan-Siberian whitefish species (*Coregonus autumnalis*) that made its way to Ireland around 15,000 years ago, it is now unique to our island.

As with salmon, eel and trout, pollan, often described as a freshwater herring, is one of the first Irish fish that was eaten by the earliest inhabitants of the island. Pollan most likely entered the Shannon, the longest river in Ireland, at the end of the last Ice Age and spread to the five loughs, all of which were interconnected at the time.

In 2018, Lough Neagh pollan was awarded EU Protected Designation of Origin (PDO) status. Lough Neagh is the only lake where pollan are fished for commercial purposes. It's a pity we don't celebrate it more. I'm sure most Irish people have never even heard of it.

According to Florence Irwin (1949), fishermen would either fry it fresh or scale, gut and dry it to use at a later date. As it was persevered, dried pollan could last indefinitely in the right conditions. The typical way of frying pollan was to gut and wash them, then roll them in flour seasoned with salt and pepper. You have to close your eyes and imagine the fishermen of Lough Neagh frying these fish in cast iron pans over fires by the side of the lough. Though those days are well and truly past, these images give us a unique lens into our food culture on the island of Ireland.

Ray

A Dublin classic according to Dublin chefs, restaurateurs and fishmongers, ray wing was once a staple in many of the fish shops in Dublin, where the combination of ray and chips was a popular order. So much ray wing was landed over the years at the Dublin fishing village of Ringsend that the area became known as Raytown (Allen 1995: 49).

Rejected in many parts of Ireland, ray wing became a staple foodstuff for the people of Ringsend from the early 19th century. It was landed as bycatch by beam trawlers. After a large haul of ray, which would be salted in the sea by being towed on lines, one resident who lived in Ringsend in 1910s recalls:

> You'd put the wings on the line between the houses of our narrow streets and after 4–5 days the drying ray would become 'pissy' (smelling strongly of ammonia). This was a distinctive smell in Ringsend. You needed to let the sun and wind get to them to dry them properly and you'd have wing for 6 months or more (Scherer 2020).

In 1790, a Frenchman visiting Kinsale observed that despite the Dublin love of ray, the local Cork fishermen discarded it, so it seems ray was not for everyone in Ireland.

Salmon

Due to a massive fall in the availability of wild salmon, farmed salmon now abounds. Ironically, many Irish people who don't eat fish will eat salmon, a phenomenon that I cannot explain (like the Irish people who don't eat meat but still eat chicken; we are a strange bunch).

There are those who swear by wild salmon. And then there are those who are happy with the farmed organic variety. Is this like the debate about cheese? Is it artisan vs. commodity all over again? The native Irish vs. the invader?

This is not the place to discuss the merits or otherwise of fish farming, especially salmon fish farming, which seems to divide people in a way not seen since the Irish Civil War. Suffice it to say that wild salmon is in short supply. We rarely see it from one year to the next. When we do secure one, I nearly always cure it due to its cost and size.

In terms of its place in our food history, salmon is one of our three central fish (the other two are trout and bass). All three have been fished since the very first people arrived in Ireland over 10,000 years ago. During the summer and autumn, hunter-gatherers at Mount Sandel in Coleraine, Co. Derry would have happily fed off the salmon swimming in the River Bann (Woodman 2015).

The salmon holds a particularly important place in Irish folklore. In Pre-Christian Ireland, the salmon was a symbol of knowledge and was said to have mystical powers, giving 'life force' to those who ate it (Mahon 1991: 42). It appears in many of our sagas and heroic tales, such as in the Fenian Cycle. In one story, the salmon eats nine hazelnuts that fall into the Well of Wisdom (*An Tobar Segais*) from nine hazel trees that surrounded the well. By eating these nuts, the salmon gained all the world's knowledge. While cooking the salmon for an older poet, Fionn Mac Cumhaill burned his thumb on the crispy fat and thereby gained all its knowledge. Fionn roasted the salmon over applewood and served it with wild watercress. I can think of no better way to serve a wild salmon nowadays to connect past traditions with present practice.

Smoked salmon is probably one of Ireland's greatest exports. From Graham and Saoirse Roberts in Connemara and Birgitta Curtin in Co. Clare to the legendary Sally Barnes in West Cork (who only smokes wild salmon), there are a multitude of artisan producers keeping the art of smoking fish in Ireland alive.

Salted ling

There is an old Gaelic saying: 'Ling would be the beef of the sea if it had salt enough, butter enough and boiling enough.'

Though not as famous as its counterpart, salted cod, salted ling has long been a staple of rural Irish fishing communities. In his 1948 essay 'The Ling in Irish Commerce', Arthur E.J. Went cites examples from 1364 (Ballycotton, Co. Cork) and 1537 (Dungarvan, Co. Waterford) of the importance of this fish. During the 17th century, ling was exported from Galway to England and Spain. According to Went, ling is 'an ancient Irish food' and 'is part of the Irish heritage'.

As with cod, ling was preserved by salting and drying the fillets. In this way, it kept for a long time. Though the practice of salting ling has all but died away due to refrigeration and freezing, it is still sometimes sold in Cork.

There was a time when you could find salted ling hanging from the roofs in country shops, especially in the South of the country. In her book *Irish Holiday* (1939), social historian Dorothy Hartley observes that salted ling hung from shop ceiling in Skerries in North Co. Dublin: 'Along the coast a lot of this good fish is salted, most is cured, and the curing is done along the west coasts of Ireland.' Famously, when the Irish playwright and poet J.M. Synge visited the Aran Islands at the turn of the 20th century, he lived off salted ling and potatoes.

Scallops

Can someone please sort out our hand-dived scallop problem? And while you're at it, our inability to buy scallops in their shells? It's all tied up in bureaucracy. I've written so much over the years about this issue in Ireland. We seem to be the only country in Europe that sells scallops out of their shells. If I want a scallop in its shell, I have to go to Scotland. Ridiculous, right?

Hand-diving for scallops was banned in the 1980s. It's said that it was due to illegal diving but I'm of the opinion that big industry had a say in the matter. Can you imagine buying an oyster out of its shell? Of course not.

Queenies (small scallops) are a common sight in the West of Ireland and can be found, when in season, at the Galway market on Saturdays. Theodora FitzGibbon includes a recipe for them fried with bacon and mushrooms in her book *Irish Traditional Food* (1983). Perhaps it's the Irish love of bacon that saves shellfish, in much the same way the Spanish combine chorizo with mussels and clams. I once heard someone on the radio say that bacon always makes things taste better. Perhaps they're right, especially when you're in Ireland.

The combination of scallops and black pudding is said to have been invented by chef Gerry Galvin in Galway. We've served this classic Irish combination in Cava Bodega, our Spanish restaurant, ever since we opened. Though the garnish often changes, we always serve it with cauliflower purée. In the autumn, we pan-fry scallops in brown butter with sage and hazelnuts.

In his essay 'The History of Seafood in Irish Cuisine and Culture' (2005: 229), chef and food historian Máirtín Mac Con Iomaire recalls that 'scallops were clearly common enough in the 1930s according to the story of a County Limerick housewife who was apologising profusely to a German engineer working on the Ard na Crusha power station that all she had for his dinner were scallops!'

Sea bass

At Mount Sandel in Co. Derry, which is Ireland's oldest known settlement, hunter-gatherers would have speared sea bass in the shallow waters of the River Bann. They would have also trapped or caught eel, salmon and trout (Woodman 2015). As I have intimated elsewhere in this book, we seem ignorant of our first foods on this island that make up the core of our Irish food story. Yes, we have beef and lamb and pork and potatoes, but these are not the main players in the long history of people and food on this island. For the first 4,000 years there were no ruminants on the island and potatoes didn't arrive until 8,600 years after the first settlers.

Though most sea bass sold in Ireland now is farmed in Greece, it is still possible to secure a wild sea bass for oneself (it is prohibited to land it and sell it commercially). All wild sea bass available in Ireland now come from France or the UK. The tragedy is that wild sea bass is caught in Irish waters and then discarded due to quotas.

Traditionally, sea bass was baked whole or braised in a fish kettle. Cider, fennel and butter are all you need to make this fish sing. The next time you bag yourself a wild sea bass, think of those first Irish settlers spearing bass in the waters of the River Bann and acknowledge the depth of the Irish food story.

Trout

For thousands of years, rivers played an important role as a food source for Irish people. Along with wild salmon and eel, brown trout provided sustenance to the earliest inhabitants of Ireland. From the first early Irish settlers to today's anglers, these same rivers still provide us with food. Most of our early settlements and subsequent towns were built next to a river, whether at its mouth or along it. This allowed communities to have a constant source of food.

Over time, we have gradually abandoned our rivers as a source of food. The issue of access to land, and the rivers that run through the land, was a contentious issue from the 16th century onwards due to the English colonisation of Ireland. This probably contributed to the amnesia that has befallen us in relation to fish like trout.

Whether potted or baked in cider, trout has a rich history of being cooked on the island, though it is rare to see it on menus nowadays. In *The Irish Sketch Book* (1900), the British novelist William M. Thackeray describes cooking trout on hot turf ashes on the floor of a cottage at Lake Derryclare in Connemara:

> Marcus, the boatman, commenced forthwith to gut the fish, and taking down some charred turf-ashes from the blazing fire, on which about a hundredweight of potatoes were boiling, he – Marcus – proceeded to grill on the floor some of the trout, which afterwards we ate with immeasurable satisfaction. They were such trouts as, when once tasted, remain for ever in recollection of a commonly grateful mind – rich, flaky, creamy, full of flavour. A Parisian gourmand would have paid ten francs each for the smallest cooleen among them [...] they were red or salmon trouts – none of you white-fleshed brown-skinned fellows.

Trout was traditionally fried in butter or rubbed with oil and placed under a grill. I love to serve it raw, though most Irish people would find this practice sacrilegious. We do not do well with raw food in Ireland.

○ 8 ○

Seaweed

Language is important. When you call something a weed, it tends to get overlooked. According to the *Online Etymology Dictionary* website, the etymology of the word *seaweed* in English goes back to at least the 16th century and denotes 'plant or plants growing in the sea'. But the word *weed* means 'plants not valued for use or beauty'.

Irish is an older language than English and points towards a more amenable position. Seaweed in Irish is *feamainn*, which means 'sea-rod'. As John Keane (2021) observes:

> The English word, seaweed, does not do justice to Ireland's richest, replenishable, sustainable resource which we have in abundance around our coasts. It certainly is not a weed. On the other hand, many Irish language words capture the essence of their subject matter in a richer, more descriptive fashion than English. This is especially true with *feamainn*, the Irish for seaweed, which reflects the important role seaweed extracts play in combatting stress in all life forms.

Archaeological evidence shows that before the arrival of the potato in Ireland, many coastal people farmed seaweed and lived quite happily on it. It is a vegetable, after all (actually, it's more of a marine algae, but let's not split hairs). Why isn't seaweed farmed more in Ireland, as it is in Japan? There are currently only a few seaweed farms in Ireland, for example kelp farmed by Kate Burns on Rathlin Island in Northern Ireland and Paul Cobb's Roaring Water Sea Vegetable Farm in Cork.

In his book *Thirty-two Words for Field*, Manchán Magan (2020: 265) writes eloquently about the importance of seaweed as a 'vital component in Irish society, providing food, fertiliser and fuel'. In winter, when the land sleeps, the sea is awake as a food source to sustain. Channelled wrack, which we pick and pickle in Aniar, was said to be at its best at Christmastime. The people of Tory Island, Magan writes, would cook the tips to make a most delicious healthy snack (2020: 268).

o8 1

Simnel cake

Simnel cake is a light fruitcake that was traditionally baked and eaten during the pre-Easter period in Ireland. It is iced with marzipan and capped by a circle of 11 balls made of the same paste. These balls symbolise the 11 apostles.

It was originally made for the fourth Sunday in Lent (which was called Simnel Sunday). Traditionally, female servants would bake this fruitcake using all the ingredients that had to be used up before the fast and abstinence of Lent. They would give the cake to their mothers when visiting on this Sunday (also called Mothering Sunday).

Darina Allen (1995) observes that the cake more than likely entered Ireland in Elizabethan times as a spiced bread and was transformed into a cake over time.

In the 'Hades' episode in James Joyce's *Ulysses* (1922), the narrator and Bloom observe: 'Beyond the hind carriage a hawker stood by his barrow of cakes and fruit. Simnel cakes those are, stuck together: cakes for the dead. Dogbiscuits. Who ate them?' Seemingly these small cakes were so hard that they reminded Joyce of dog food as opposed to cakes for humans.

082

Soft drinks

My nana (and many other Irish people) calls soft drinks *minerals*. 'Would you have a mineral?' she would ask when we sat down in the Strand Hotel in Bray. She would bring all us grandkids to the bookies to take the yellow paper and pencils so we would have something to draw on, then we'd go over to the Strand to have a glass of Club Orange, Britvic or 7up. In the shops my nana would pick up some knock-off of Coca-Cola, usually one with a white thrift label wrapped around the bottle. This was all part of the Irish food story for a young boy growing up in the 1980s.

Other soft drinks that I remember were Lilt (a sparkling pineapple drink) and Orangina (first developed in Algeria in 1933), but many others have been lost to time. Does anyone remember Cavan Cola? It was a regional cola made in Cavan from 1953 that went nationwide in 1990. You can still see the slightly twee TV advertisement on YouTube. What about Cadet, those little sugar-filled bottles that found their way into the goodie bags at kids' birthday parties during the 1980s?

Or what about Tanora? Was it only Cork people who drank this? In his play *Disco Pigs*, Enda Walsh has one of the characters order 'Two Battur burgurs! Two Sauce! Two Chips! Two Peas! Two Tanora!' (Walsh 1997: 12). When the famous Irish footballer Denis Irwin was playing for Manchester United, his mother would send him a large bottle of Tanora and packs of Tayto crisps from Cork.

Before globalisation arrived in Ireland with a bang in the mid-1990s, there were many regional Irish soft drinks. Did we just give up on them? Or were their American or British counterparts better? Does it come down again to our lack of appreciation of our own food and drink culture?

One soft drink company, Dwan Drinks, based in Thurles, Co. Tipperary, which manufactured soft drinks from 1921, has recently been reinvented as a microbrewery by the grandson of the original owner. This is what the Irish food story is all about: a constant flux of realisation and reinvention. While many of these soft drinks may now be lost to history, others re-emerge anew, ready to change our minds again regarding food and drink in Ireland.

Football Special

Ireland suffers from the perception that there is a lack of regionality when it comes to our food and drink. While this is not the case, many Irish people struggle to define regional foodstuffs. However, one of the most well-known is a Donegal drink called Football Special.

Football Special began its life as a celebratory drink to honour the successes of the Swilly Rovers, a Donegal football club. The drink was originally called Football Cup and was produced by the McDaid family. It was designed for players to fill the cup with a non-alcoholic beverage after winning a match.

During the early 20th century, Guinness used local bottlers to finish and bottle Guinness. These 'bottlers' then distributed Guinness throughout the locality. In 1958, the McDaid family was awarded a bottling contract from Guinness. A tank of brewed Guinness would be delivered, then the McDaid family would ferment and bottle this product at the quay in Ramelton before distributing it to all the pubs in North Donegal.

During their years bottling for Guinness, the McDaid family learned about the technology involved and applied this to soft drinks production. Soon an old creamery was bought in Ramelton, which had its own spring water source, and a small soft drinks factory was established and used to develop a unique range of drinks, including Football Special.

The McDaid family is still in business to this day – now in their fourth generation – with many more products added to their portfolio, such as ice cream. With the nostalgia that surrounds this drink, there is now an international demand for it.

For Mia Cummins Greaves in Tipperary, if anyone went to Donegal, a big treat was 'to bring me back some Football Special'. It was a 'Donegal thing'.

It was the first time I tasted food and realised it was not only about eating. I realised that food came from somewhere and that it had its own culture. That it was its own world. I realised that the type of food you eat can define you, for better or worse. It was a marker, a status symbol.

083
Spaghetti Bolognese

My first food epiphany occurred in Cashel, Co. Tipperary. I was a young boy, sitting with my family in a restaurant called Chez Hans in the 1980s. My eyes fell upon a dish called spaghetti Bolognese. I don't recall knowing what it was, but told my mother that that was what I was having. 'You won't like it,' she said, but I persisted.

When it arrived, it had a strange sprig of something green on top. I tasted it. It was bitter and faintly aromatic (it was parsley). To my mother's amazement, I ate everything.

It might seem trite now (it's comical to my kids), but it was the first time I tasted food and realised it was not only about eating. I realised that food came from somewhere and that it had its own culture. That it was its own world. I realised that the type of food you eat can define you, for better or worse. It was a marker, a status symbol. This was the start of my food journey, my journey into food on this island, my journey into Irish food. Thus, food in Ireland became part of the story of Irish food, irrespective of its own culinary origins.

Italian rocket also whirled into Ireland with a vengeance in the 1990s. It seems to have replaced the iceberg and butterhead lettuce that were a staple of many an Irish teatime in the 1980s. Coupled with sun-dried tomatoes and a ball of mozzarella, it captured the new spirit of Ireland: out with the bacon and cabbage, in with the chicken breast or pasta dish with rocket. The fact that taken together, the three ingredients – rocket, chicken, sun-dried tomatoes – almost resemble the colours of the Irish flag helped this trio to take hold of our fledging food consciousness in the boom time of the later 1990s.

I saw that Italian food, and later Spanish food, could teach us how to build our own food culture, our own food story. It was not about reinventing the wheel; it was about learning from other countries that were better at telling their story. It wasn't that we didn't have a food story: we just didn't know how to tell it.

o84

Spice bag

Truth be told, I have never had a spice bag. My teenage daughter and her entire generation love them. Ordering one for her recently in a local takeaway, a man approached me and said, 'So this is where the Michelin-star chefs eat.' I tried to explain to him that it was for my daughter, but he wasn't having it.

The spice bag is another unique and curious Irish fusion food, like the 3-in-1 (chips, curry and rice) and lasagne, coleslaw and chips. A spice bag (which can also be called a spice box) usually consists of a bag of deep-fried chicken (which can be shredded, wings or balls), chips, red and green peppers, chilli peppers and plenty of spices. In some cases it can also include pork and fried onions. There is also a seafood one (with prawns) and a vegetarian one.

The spice bag began to appear in Ireland in 2010. According to RTÉ reporter Liam Geraghty, it was created by The Sunflower Chinese takeaway in Templeogue, Co. Dublin. For this reason, it's seen as a fusion of Irish and Chinese 'takeaway' cuisine. In 2017, at the Just Eat National Takeaway Awards, the spice bag was voted Ireland's favourite takeaway food (Digby 2021).

Irish chefs from Karl Whelan to Kwanghi Chan have since offered up their own more sophisticated versions, but the dish is still resolutely in the fast food lane in Ireland. Whether you love it or loathe it, the spice bag now has a place in the Irish food story and is as Irish as soda bread or lamb stew.

o8 5

Stout

While it may be unfair to only mention Guinness as the stout that made the Irish, it certainly contributed to the image of the Irish as a stout-loving people (and a drink-loving one at that). But why did we see stout as an essential part of Irishness, of being Irish? Stout began its life in England, after all, as did many other Irish things.

Black beer (*leann dubh*) was born in London in the early 18th century. The first known use of the word *stout* in relation to beer occurs in a document dated from 1677 in the Egerton Manuscripts in the British Library and referred to the strength of the beer. The word *porter*, meanwhile, comes from the fact that the beer was popular with porters in England in the 1720s.

Stout's association with Ireland, mostly through Guinness (est. 1759) but also though Beamish (est. 1792) and Murphy's (est. 1856), made me want to further explore its history and its relationship to the food it was served with and the places it was served in. Though stout began its life in England, it is the drier version of stout that we now associate with Ireland.

Beef and Guinness stew is an 18th-century dish that has become one of the icons of Irish food. Stout and oysters are a now a classic Irish pairing, but the origins of the combination are obscure (see page 158). One story is that they were considered a poor man's man lunch in Dublin. Oysters would often be added to a beef and stout pie to plump up the filling. Another story locates the origin of the combination in Galway. Oyster stout, which is actually made with a small number of oysters, is a fascinating historical stout that is now being produced again.

Stout butter, a reduction of stout whipped into butter, is a recent discovery that pairs amazingly well with Irish soda bread. Stout still plays a central role in the flavour profile of the food we produce and in the story of Irish food.

o 8 6
Strawberries

Irish strawberries will forever be sold on the side of the road in my imagination. To my mind, they are an essential part of the Irish food experience. The next time you see a roadside stand selling Wexford strawberries, stop and enjoy a little box of them, closing your eyes to savour the intense sweetness of an Irish summer locked into this little red fruit.

When you consider that 10 million tonnes of strawberries are produced globally every year, it's surprising that the garden strawberry (the one we all know) did not exist before the 18th century. The emergence of the cultivated garden strawberry came from breeding the wild Chilean strawberry (*Fragaria chiloensis*) with a North American variety (*Fragaria virginiana*).

Before that, it was only the wild woodland variety that people enjoyed with their whipped cream, a combination said to have been created by Cardinal Thomas Wolsey for Henry VIII in the 16th century. Evidence of wild strawberry consumption during the Viking age (over 1,000 years ago) has been uncovered in Fishamble Street in Dublin.

Wild strawberries seem harder and harder to find nowadays, though they were once as common as blackberries in the hedgerows along many a boreen. The loss of many hedgerows due to our increasingly more intensive agricultural system has led to a reduction in the number of wild strawberries. If you do find them, appreciate them, as these wild little morsels may not be around for too much longer.

087

Sugar sandwich

It's as simple as it sounds. Take two slices of bread, butter them, sprinkle with brown or white sugar, sandwich together, cut in half and there you have it: my school lunch as a boy.

Growing up I thought it was just my family that ate sugar sandwiches. In 2019, when I included them in my play *Irish Food. A Play*, which premiered at the Dublin Fringe Festival, many people came up to me after the play was performed and told me their own sugar sandwich story. A couple from Poland even told me that they had eaten them as kids. So maybe it wasn't just us in Ireland. Perhaps all of Europe was doing it. Perhaps we were more European than we thought we were way back in the 1970s and 1980s.

o88

Swede

Are all swedes turnips or are all turnips swedes? At what point in our 10,000-year food history did swedes, those large rutabagas, surreptitiously acquire the name of those small, tender white taproots? So once and for all, let's call it as it is: a turnip is small and delicate and white, while a swede is large and rough and yellow.

The word *turnip* is a compound of the words *turn* and *neep*, derived from the Latin *napus*, the word for the plant. The word *rutabaga*, on the other hand, comes from the Swedish dialectal word *rotabagge*, from *root* and *bagge* ('lump' and 'bunch', respectively). A rutabaga, the common name for a swede in North America, is a Swedish turnip, hence the name *swede*.

Mashed turnip made a frequent appearance in the winter dinners of my youth. I don't think I ever saw an actual turnip until I worked in restaurants. When a French chef told me you could eat turnips raw, I failed to imagine how he could get one of the massive yellow swedes into his mouth. Little did I know his turnip was small and elegant, unlike mine. Nowadays, turnips are common enough in Ireland and feature on many summer menus.

o89

Swiss roll

There was a time in Ireland when everyone was Swiss roll mad. There were even competitions for the best Swiss roll. As Vanessa Greenwood (2018) writes, 'Even people who have no interest in baking often lament the demise of the Swiss roll.'

My sister tells me I spent much of my 1994 Junior Cert year making Swiss rolls to practise for my final exam. I recall making one, but I don't remember making so many. I still occasionally make a Swiss roll with jam and cream.

Ironically, Swiss roll doesn't come from Switzerland. It probably originated in Slovenia or Austria, which is why it goes by so many different names around the world: jelly roll in the US, *gâteau roulé* in France, *biskuitrolle* in Germany and *brazo gitano* in Spain. The earliest reference to it in England dates from 1842.

It's funny how food travels through time as well as place. When I sit down to eat it, I imagine I'm in my grandma's in Mount Merrion in Co. Dublin, eating a slice of a freshly baked Swiss roll that she had purchased from the local bakery near her house, served exquisitely on her little china plates.

○ 9 ○

Tea

For playwright John B. Keane, writing in his short food book *Strong Tea* (1963: 10):

> We are a nation of idealists. We are a nation of poets and we are a nation of conversationalists. We are a nation of die-hards and I will go so far as to say that we are a nations of realists, but we are first and foremost a nation of tea drinkers, and it could be said that the hand which holds the teapot rules the country.

Tea arrived in Ireland in the early part of the 18th century. Before tea became our premier beverage, buttermilk was the go-to drink for many a famished man (or woman) cutting turf in the bog.

As with coffee and chocolate, tea was first enjoyed by the wealthy for nearly a century before it became a staple of the Irish culinary imagination. At the outset, the tea party was the preserve of the rich landed class. Tea only reached Donegal around 1890 (Creedon 2022: 123). Little did they know what would happen next.

At the turn of the 20th century, the rural Irish depended on two main products for sustenance: white bread and tea. Of course, they also ate eggs, milk and other products, but these two new commodities dominated the Irish diet just as the potato had done a century earlier.

Excessive tea-drinking promoted a new 'moral panic' regarding the Irish diet. Many saw tea as a stimulant with no nutritional value, only to be used for 'purposes of exhilaration and hedonism' (Miller 2015: 324). By 1904, many considered tea-drinking to be out of control, sending some to the asylum (Clarkson and Crawford 2001). Though it's hard to understand this now, the debate at the time was a serious one, with many people abstaining for fear of becoming a 'tea drunkard.'

Tea consumption finally came under control and we returned to being worried about other things, such as our consumption of alcohol.

My first cup of tea as a young boy was a rite of passage. I was in my friend's bedroom, having tea and toast. I felt like James Dean in *Rebel without a Cause*. We were rulebreakers. We were tea drinkers. Of course, our tea was very milky. Milky tea was for the children who couldn't take the tannin in a regular cup of tea, so we were still just kids after all. Sinead O'Donnell-Carey in Donegal says, 'I loved racing home from school in the 1980s. My childminder used to make me four slices of brown bread toast with real butter and milky tea while I watched *The Brady Bunch*.'

Perhaps the most serious tea question nowadays is whether you drink Barry's or Lyons. Each Irish family has their own favourite brand.

A word on herbal tea is needed, as it probably represents a longer 'tea' tradition in Ireland. We can well imagine the Iron Age settlers steeping nettles in water to make a refreshing, nutritious drink. We make such wild infusions in Aniar, though we wouldn't call them tea. We use them for the base of our non-alcoholic drink pairings in the restaurant, turning them into juices and kombuchas. Perhaps the current craze for kombucha will soon find its way into the Irish food story if it hasn't already.

Solaris Tea, a company that produces herbal, green and other tea, is based in Galway city. Their founder, Jörg Müller, is a trained herbalist. I have had the pleasure of foraging with him on a number of occasions and his knowledge of the nutritional aspects of wild plants is astounding. Jörg's ability to make teas from wild herbs, fruits and flowers shows yet another side to the Irish food story.

091

Toasties

....

My favourite food pairing for Pinot Noir is a good ham and cheese toastie. I expect regular sliced pan, basic ham and even more basic cheese. Perhaps a few slices of tomato, sliced red onion and a smidgen of mayonnaise. However, I could just as easily go full local and get a wedge of sourdough with the best possible ham and some great Irish farmhouse Cheddar, such as Hegarty's or Coolattin. That's the thing about toasties: you can see both sides of a food culture inside them.

Pub ham and cheese toasties are something to savour. My go-to place for a toastie and a glass of wine is the Bunch of Grapes pub in Galway. There's nothing fancy about it, but it's what I want when I want to relax, when I just want something with a little bit of heart and love. Sometimes it can be found in the simplest and most basic of things. Sometimes it's about the people, about what everyone is eating: the commensality of food. That's also part of the Irish food story. So if you're looking for an insight into Irish food, from Malin Head to Mizen Head, go in search of an Irish pub that does ham and cheese toasties.

Tasty Toasty, located in the Galway bus station, are serving perhaps the finest ham and cheese toasties (made with sourdough and farmhouse cheese from Sheridans) in the West of Ireland. Eating them is an experience that makes me proud to see how far we have come to make a simple toastie a vital part of the Irish food story.

092

Tuna & sweetcorn

Who put tuna and sweetcorn together? And why do the Irish love it so much? You can be assured that at every sandwich bar in every petrol station and deli in Ireland, you will be able to avail of this option. Tinned tuna, mayonnaise and sweetcorn, on brown or white bread. An Irish classic if there ever was one.

Nowadays, we are entirely gentrified in the West of Ireland and enjoy the occasional bluefin tuna raw, sashimi-style, or simply dressed with cold-pressed rapeseed oil and preserved fruits. We are far from the land of sweetcorn. But those sandwiches still abound lest we forget who we are. We may have notions now, but there will always be tuna and sweetcorn sandwiches.

Though the Europeans have a penchant for putting premium fish into tins, most tinned fish sold in Ireland is not known for its delectable quality. However, Shines, a family-owned company fishing out of Killybegs, produces a wonderful wild Irish tuna in olive oil in tins and jars. The tuna is an albacore tuna that is fished in Irish waters from July to September. They also produce tinned mackerel and sardines. Perhaps there is hope yet for tinned fish in future stories of Irish food?

°93
Tutti-frutti

Though most of us would associate the word *tutti-frutti* with the colourful confectionery or the flavour of an ice cream, it's also the name of a fruit compote in the Netherlands. Somehow this compote made its way to Donegal and a recipe from Eileen Lawlor of Ballyshannon, Co. Donegal was included in Theodora FitzGibbon's *Irish Traditional Food* (1983). The recipe includes a smorgasbord of fruit – rhubarb, oranges, dried apricots, prunes, dried figs, lemon and apples – as well as cloves, almonds and sugar. The fruit was allowed to sit together overnight, then boiled to a pulp. The pips, stones and rinds were removed, then it was cooked again with an equal quantity of sugar. It's more of a jam than a compote, and a strange one indeed from a little town in Donegal.

094

Viennetta

Viennetta is an ice cream cake made of soft ice cream and crisp layers of chocolate that overlap and are frozen together. The ice cream pattern that is piped in a concertina pattern is actually trademarked. 'One slice is never enough,' said the voice on the TV advertisement. How could old Irish desserts compete with this?

They couldn't, as far as us kids were concerned. We thought a Viennetta was the height of luxury. We always pressured our parents to buy one for dessert on a Friday or Saturday. Looking back, I know now it was all marketing and sugar.

Viennetta still exists. Though many Irish pastry chefs have attempted to recreate this dessert in their own restaurants, the results are always a little saddening. 'The past is a foreign country,' as L.P. Hartley wrote in his book *The Go-Between* (1953). 'They do things differently there.' For me, the Viennetta is best left in the past and remembered for what it was for us as kids. Sometimes our food memories cloud our judgment and thwart our ability to see the past clearly. Looking back is easier than looking forward because that time is over.

095

Watercress

Like many wild plants, watercress seems to hide in plain sight in our rivers and streams. It is a truly ancient Irish herb. In fact, it's one of the oldest known leaf herbs consumed by humans.

Watercress is an aquatic flowering plant. Even though most of the watercress we now consume is farmed, plenty can still be found in rivers around Ireland. Of course, you need to know that the river is clean and the watercress must always be cut above the water line. But that's not to say you shouldn't go out and look. Few wild plants that are still so readily accessible can directly connect you with Ireland the way watercress can.

It was customary for monks to grow watercress in the ponds and rivers of monastery gardens. During the golden age in Ireland (between the coming of Christianity in the 5th century and the arrival of the Viking invaders in the 9th century), watercress was regularly used to make soups or pottages along with barley, nettles and other herbs. In times of abstinence, it was eaten with dry bread and boiled salmon (Mahon 1990: 106).

Younger watercress is good in a salad or as a garnish, whereas older leaves are better for soups or purée. I prefer to make a purée and then turn it into a soup if needed, as opposed to the other way around. The purée can be frozen for up to six months and can be combined with nettles, spinach, ground elder or nasturtium. Watercress was often used in egg sandwiches in Ireland in the past, but it seems to have been replaced with rocket nowadays.

096

Wheat

Agriculture proper has its beginnings in Ireland around 3,800 years ago at sites such as the Céide Fields in Co. Mayo, one of the oldest Neolithic field systems in the world. This site is made up of small fields partitioned by dry-stone walls. The Céide Fields were farmed for several centuries between 3700 and 3200 BC. For those who think Ireland has no food history, we need only imagine some of the first famers ploughing this rough terrain, growing barley, rye and wheats such as emmer and einkorn thousands of years ago.

Innovations of 'Celtic' civilisation in Ireland include thrown-wheel pottery as well as rotary stones for grinding wheat. Emmer and einkorn are still available today but are little used in Irish baking. The Iron Age diet revolved around wheat porridges, also made from barley or oats. Whole hulled wheat could be boiled in milk, as could barley (Mahon 1991: 65). This tradition continued up until the 19th century, when the oat porridge that we know today (which itself has a long history in Ireland, dating back thousands of years; see page 102) replaced it altogether.

However, due to the damp weather, Ireland's climate was not suitable for growing wheat on a large scale, so wheat bread was not a staple until the introduction of white bread in the 19th century. Up until that point, only the nobility got to eat wheaten bread. From the 12th century, the Norman barons and wealthy merchants who surrounded them were known to serve bread of the finest quality with their meat and fish course (Mahon 1991: 71).

Trenchers were thick slices of bread made with wholemeal flour that were a few days old. They were served on a silver or pewter platter and used almost like plates; the sauce for the fish and meat would be absorbed into them. At the end of the banquet, they were collected and given to the servants or the dogs.

09 7
Whiskey

The word *whiskey* has its roots in the Irish language. The fact that the Irish for whiskey, *uisce beatha*, translates as 'the water of life' says a lot about our eating and drinking habits. If you drink this, you won't need food. Eating is cheating, as the old saying goes.

It was said in the past that an Irishman would crawl over 'the naked bodies of ten beautiful women' just to get a bottle of whiskey, though I'm not sure we're allowed to write such things anymore (Hickey 2018: 269). Queen Elizabeth I once said that whiskey was her only Irish friend.

The Irish climate is perfect for making whiskey. All you need is Irish barley, water, yeast and time. Indeed, barley, which arrived in Ireland around 3500 BC, is the soul of whiskey.

Whiskey in Ireland takes at least three years to make and it matures in wood casks. From three distilleries for most of the 20th century, the island of Ireland (including Northern Ireland) now has over 50.

Though the first written mention of whiskey dates to 1405 and appears in *The Annals of the Four Masters*, the process of making whiskey was most likely brought to Ireland by monks around 1000 AD. However, whiskey made in this period was not aged and contained dried fruit (raisins and dates) as well as herbs and spices (aniseed, liquorice, thyme and mint).

By 1556, whiskey was widespread. An Act passed by the English Parliament declared whiskey to be 'a drink nothing profitable to be drunken daily and used, is now universally throughout this realm made' (Lees 1864: 54).

Presently, there are four types of Irish whiskey: single malt, single grain, single pot still and blended. Single malt is whiskey made entirely from malted barley and produced in one distillery. Single grain is made from any combination of cereal grains and is distilled in a column still with no more than 30% malted barley. Single pot still is the only uniquely Irish style of whiskey. Made only in Ireland, it contains a minimum of 30% malted barley and a minimum of 30% unmalted barley.

Blended Irish whiskey combines single grain with single malt whiskeys as well as single pot still Irish whiskey. Thus, a combination of malted and unmalted barely is blended to make a whiskey with a lighter palate, nose and aroma. The definition for blended Irish whiskey was coined in the 19th century by Dublin Distillers to make a more approachable whiskey that would appeal to a wider market.

Whiskey cream liqueurs are also popular in Ireland, with Baileys being the best-known. However, combing whiskey with cream (and oatmeal and honey) has been part of the Irish food story for centuries (see 'Scalteen' below).

At Aniar, we make many whiskey infusions or liquors by adding wild fruits, herbs and nuts, such as rosehips or hazelnuts, to whiskey and other spirits. While most Irish people will recognise this practice in terms of sloe gin, blackcurrant whiskey was another common drink and appears in the manuscript of Mary Ponsonby from around 1850 (Allen 1995: 324).

Perhaps the strangest infusion I've made to date was a roasted chicken skin whiskey. I got the idea when someone said to me, 'How come we can put whiskey in your chicken sauce but we can't put chicken in our whiskey?' As bizarre as it sounds, the practice of fat-washing whiskey (adding animal fat to whiskey to flavour it), particularly with lamb fat, was quite common in Ireland historically. As the fat and the whiskey wouldn't bind, they could be separated after the flavour of the fat had been imparted. Fat gives a roundness to whiskey – brown butter is now used in many whiskey cocktails in Ireland.

Irish coffee

Irish coffee is said to have been invented by Joe Sheridan in Foynes, Co. Limerick, in the 1940s, when transatlantic flights recommenced after World War Two. Sheridan was head chef at the restaurant and coffee shop in the Foynes Airbase flying boat terminal (which is 15km from present-day Shannon Airport). Sometime in the early 1940s, he added whiskey to the coffee for disembarking Pan Am passengers who had had a particularly bumpy flight.

However, a combination of whiskey with coffee as a cocktail has been part of both Irish and European culture for much longer. In 19th-century Vienna, for example, coffeehouses served coffee cocktails topped with cream. A 'gloria' was a coffee and spirit drink mentioned in the novels of both Balzac and Flaubert. Yet the phenomena that we know today certainly began its life in Ireland in the 1940s and has since become an icon of Irish drink and culture.

> In 1952, cases of Irish whiskey were shipped to a Council of Europe meeting in Strasbourg where the Irish secretariat showcased Irish whiskey as 'the best in the world'. Bottles accompanied by a recipe for how to make Irish coffee were distributed to delegates at Strasbourg (Houlihan 2023).

By 1957, Irish coffee was introduced to Las Vegas by an early version of Enterprise Ireland, where they were making around 1,000 coffees a week. After drinking an Irish coffee in Los Angeles in 1957, the American actor Danny Kaye, who starred in *White Christmas* (1954), said 'there's nothing funny about this drink, it's nectar' (cited in Houlihan 2023).

Irish coffee, alongside Irish stew, is probably one of the first things to come to mind when people are asked about the food and drink of Ireland. However, on the international circuit, Irish coffee competes with a range of spirit coffees, such as Russian coffee (vodka), Mexican coffee (tequila) and Jamaican coffee (rum). Perhaps it's the 'luck of the Irish' that made Irish coffee stand out worldwide.

Scalteen

Scalteen is an Irish whiskey drink made with honey and cream. In her book *Cooking at Ballymaloe House* (2000), Myrtle Allen observes that the drink is referred to in *The Diaries of Humphrey O'Sullivan*, an account written by a Kilkenny schoolteacher in the 1830s. A different recipe appears in Diarmuid Ó Muirithe's book *Words We Don't Use (Much Anymore)* (2011), attributed to a man from Tipperary: 'Add half a bottle of whiskey, two whisked eggs and a lump of butter to a pint and a half of strained beef broth to which salt and black pepper has been added. Heat the mixture well but do not boil.' Allen's is more of an after-dinner drink, while the latter seems to be more like a meal.

098

Wild game

For me, the phrase *wild game* encapsulates everything that lives without human assistance. In this way, it's the opposite of farming to a certain degree. However, there are plenty of in-between spaces, such as managing wild livestock like game birds, deer or even native oysters. These live wild, but many people believe the human intervention reduces their 'wildness'. While I don't agree with this position, I can see their point.

However, I do believe wild game should be a much bigger part of our food story than it is now. Though it has become fashionable to hunt and fish and subsequently put these items on your menu (and in your social media posts), this phenomenon has yet to permeate into the public consciousness at a wider level. On any given day, it is still difficult to find venison or mallard in a shop or supermarket in Ireland. There are a few shops around Ireland that sell wild food, but until we're all buying rabbit again – or putting it on our menus, at the very least – wild game will remain a minor aspect of the Irish food story.

Theoretically, we are much closer to understanding our natural environment than ever before. Sadly, on a practical level, we are in a worse position. The first Irish settlers who hunted wild game did so out of necessity. We stand at a crossroads in terms of adopting more wild game into the Irish food story and into the cultural experience of food on this island. It is not clear which way we will turn.

Grouse

As with other wild animals in Ireland, grouse are now rare due to years of overshooting and poor land management. Grouse feed on heather, so any loss of peatlands also leads to a decline in their number.

Grouse season begins in September in Ireland and lasts for only one month due to their small numbers. Unless you know a hunter, it's a rare bird to see on menus these days. However, grouse bones were uncovered at Ferriter's Cove in Co. Kerry, which is both a Mesolithic and Neolithic site, so they are an important part of our historic food story. In *The Irish Cookbook* (McMahon 2020), I included two recipes for grouse: one with a savoury oat porridge (to evoke the first Neolithic farmers) and another with poitín.

Hare

The Irish brown hare is the only native land animal on the island of Ireland. Though rarely eaten nowadays, they were an important food source for early Mesolithic Irish settlers right up to the mid-20th century. Initially, they were probably roasted over an open fire or smoked and dried for later. As time when on and pots became a thing, the hare made its ways into broths and soups, while its blood was added for richness and flavour.

There is archaeological evidence to suggest that the hare was one of the most hunted animals in Celtic Ireland. The Celts also held some bizarre beliefs about the hare while admiring it for its strength, speed and agility. In Celtic mythology and folklore, the hare has links to the mysterious otherworld of the supernatural. Shapeshifters were often said to take the form of a hare or lost souls would come back as a hare.

There is a legend that the Celtic warrior Oisín hunted a hare, wounding it in the leg. Oisín followed the wounded animal into a thicket, where he found a door leading down into the ground. He went in and came to a large hall, where he found a beautiful young woman sitting on a throne, bleeding from a leg wound. In the Middle Ages, witches were said to turn into hares at night and drink the milk from cows.

These are a few of the reasons, among many, that the rural poor shied away from eating hare. But that is not to say they didn't eat it. Along with rabbit, hare was an important food source for many people in medieval Ireland. Jugged hare (a kind of casserole that includes the blood of the hare) was a popular dish from the 17th century to the early 20th century. Hare pies, as well as potted hare, which used the legs of the older animal, were a feature of Anglo-Irish cooking – there are a number of manuscript recipes for them in the National Library of Ireland. A pâté would also have been made from the liver of the hares.

The season for brown hare runs from September to February, though our Aniar hunter tells me he never hunts them due to their 'special' quality (this may be linked to customs and superstitions). Though many dislike its rich, gamey flavour, eating hare provides us with a direct link to out ancient ancestors. Occasionally, seaweed-eating hares are spotted in Co. Mayo. This may be due to the lack of edible grass there or the fact that the hare has realised the rich potential of seaweed as a superfood. We could learn a little from this elegant animal.

Partridge

As with grouse, partridges are now rare in Ireland. In fact, they almost went extinct – their numbers were down to only 50 pairs in the 1900s. While the grey partridge is now found only in Offaly, the red-legged partridge (also called the French partridge), the one that is most often hunted, was introduced to Ireland specifically for game hunting. The season for hunting runs from 1 November to 31 January. They are usually found in Meath, Kildare and Wexford. They are rare out west and prefer the boglands of middle Ireland.

Pheasant

Even though we imagine ourselves to be a classless society in Ireland, pheasant and much game would certainly have been limited to people with land in the last few hundred years. But this wasn't always the case.

Game was important for all types of people for thousands of years in Ireland, from the native Irish to the Normans and beyond. It featured in plenty of medieval banquets alongside other birds such as 'snipe, woodcock, [...] partridge, and plover' (Mahon 1991: 115). In his *An Itinerary*, the Elizabethan traveller Feynes Moryson (1617) wrote, 'Ireland hath great plenty of Pheasants, and I have known sixite served at one feast.' However, he also observed that Ireland 'hath great plenty of Birds and Fowles, but by reason of their naturall sloth, they had little delight or skill in Birding or Fowling.' (He may have been biased towards the English Protestant way of life that was then being planted in many parts of the country.)

Pheasant and other game did become the preserve of the planted classes for much of the following 300 or 400 years. Pheasant soup seems to have been a favourite of this class; no one I ask has ever had it. However, over the course of the 20th century, there were plenty of families 'down the country' who shot their own pheasant. For Theresa Kane from Co. Wexford, a particular memory is of 'pheasants hanging outside the back door by the neck until they fell away and then boiled until grey.'

The first time I plucked a pheasant was for Christmas dinner. I decided that I was going to make pheasant terrine for the starter and ordered two whole pheasants. Gutting them was memorable, especially the smell, whereas I can't remember the terrine at all. I have always wanted to get to grips with whole animals and birds, so out in the garage in the cold, I eviscerated the birds while the others drank wine. Why on earth do I do these things, I remember asking myself. For food, for curiosity, is all I can answer.

Venison

One of the many questions I get asked about the Irish Famine is why the people didn't just eat wild animals. The saying 'God sent the potato blight, but the English caused the Famine' goes some way to explain the difficulty of finding food during that time, even in the wild.

During the Famine, plenty of food was exported out of Ireland and the food that was left was unavailable to the native Irish. Because most native Irish people were dispossessed in terms of land, they couldn't gain access to either the materials or the land for hunting. This may be why we have such an aversion to venison and other game in Ireland – it's a deep-seated trauma in our collective unconscious. Our ongoing attitude to wild food typifies this issue.

The word *venison* derives from the Latin *venari* ('to hunt or pursue'). The word was originally applied to all wild game, including rabbits, hares and wild pigs, but now it applies only to deer. The Romans introduced fallow deer to Britain specifically for hunting. Due to the extinction of the Irish elk, reindeer and red deer, no deer were present in Ireland when the first settlers arrived around 10,000 years ago. Red deer were introduced to Ireland by Neolithic hunters around 3500 BC and have been part of Irish food culture ever since. Fallow deer were introduced to Ireland in Norman times and sika deer (originally from Asia) were introduced to the Powerscourt Estate in the 19th century. They subsequently escaped from captivity and now number about 20,000.

Nowadays, deer farms supply Northern Ireland and England with venison all year round, but the wild variety is available only from late autumn to late winter. It's a special time of year, when venison complements many other foods that are in season then, from mushrooms to berries and nuts.

Historically, before the advent of the refrigerator, the meat would have been rubbed with ginger and black pepper to keep flies away. In a 1605 recipe, the author recommended a thick rye and lard pastry to enclose slowly cooked venison meat that was spiced with ginger and cinnamon. Spices and venison have gone hand in hand for centuries in Ireland. Venison stew has long been popular in Ireland, appearing in many recipe collections from the 19th and 20th centuries. Spiced venison pies were popular from the Middle Ages up to the 19th century. It's unfortunate that we seem to have abandoned the pie as an Irish foodstuff after independence, but I think its resurgence in recent years demonstrates the Irish love of pies (*see also* 'Dingle pie', page 59).

Despite its historic affiliations with the nobility, venison now appears to be enjoyed by many and can be found in supermarkets around Ireland. Let's hope future generations integrate it better into their own Irish food story.

Woodcock & snipe

While these two birds are not the same, they have a similar appearance. Snipe has longer legs than a woodcock and a slightly longer beak. The reason for grouping them together is that both are rare – the woodcock and the great snipe are now protected, so woodcock can no longer be hunted commercially in Ireland. Yet there was a time, many years ago, when we had both on the menu in Aniar. I feel it's important to include them here as something that we used to eat in Ireland.

According to Theodora FitzGibbon (1968), snipe cooked over a turf fire was a common way to cook them. One had to skin the bird before cutting off the wings and head, then remove the skin from the breast. Both snipe and woodcock are cooked without being drawn, which means they are cooked with their innards and digestive tract intact. I ate woodcock innards once – I was told to use them as a sauce – but I can't say it was a pleasant experience. Gnarly would be a better word.

099
Wild plants

Wild things are first things – the things that were mostly here before us, that we learned to live with and eat to sustain us. Ireland has a longer association with wild food than you might imagine – people lived on the island of Ireland for nearly 5,000 years before the advent of farming.

My experience of wild food mostly dates to after we opened Aniar restaurant in Galway in 2011. I did not grow up foraging the land. When asked by a German friend who drank cold nettle tea when he was a sick child what I had as a child when illness beset me, I replied, 'Flat 7up and HB vanilla ice cream,' illustrating my own disconnect with our native flora.

However, when we opened our restaurant Cava in 2008, we would be visited by mushroom foragers (mainly non-Irish) who would sell us everything from ceps and chanterelles to hedgehog mushrooms. Even after all this time I would say that I am only an occasional forager, even though my knowledge of our native edible plants is now quite comprehensive.

Wild food is perhaps the closest thing that connects us to our local landscape. Its importance in our current eco-centric age cannot be overlooked if we really want to reconnect with nature. (For a more detailed list of Irish wild food, see the index of wild plants, seaweed and fungi in *The Irish Cookbook* (McMahon 2020).)

Alexanders

Alexanders are a wild green edible that have been growing in Ireland since at least 1500 BC. It has a taste somewhere between celery and parsley. It also goes by the name horse parsley. It was common in the gardens of monastic settlements, especially before the introduction of celery into Ireland in the 18th and 19th centuries.

Alexanders aren't used much nowadays. With the introduction of celery, the heady days of this wild herb were numbered. I love its celery-scented flavour and its bright yellow-green flower heads. Its leaves are distinctly shiny, which helps to identify it among the other umbellifers.

In terms of eating, the whole plant is up for grabs. From its leaves (pickled or added to salads), stalks and hollow shoots (blanched as any vegetable or pickled) to its buds (beautiful when grilled over charcoal), it is a little paradise for the cook. In the autumn, you can dry the seeds and use them as a substitute for pepper or mix them with salt for a celery-tasting seasoning. You can use the plant to flavour stocks. Drying the leaves and blending them produces a lovely aromatic powder. Alexanders sugar in strawberry jam, a meringue or marshmallows is a nice touch. As with many wild herbs, it can be added to different spirits, such as vodka and gin, to make a flavoured liqueur.

Alexanders, as with many other wild herbs that grow on the island of Ireland, offer us possibilities to both explore our surrounding landscape and to investigate the history of its use on the island of Ireland. They are a true wonder and have changed my culinary life.

Blackberries

We all have a forager inside us. Why? Because we can all recognise a blackberry. Blackberry-picking is not as popular as it used to be – even when I was a child, it was on the wane. But that is not to say we can't revive past traditions for future generations.

The blackberry has a special place in Irish food and folk culture. With most of our kids (or grandkids) glued to a smartphone, it's a good time to teach them what a blackberry looks like, tastes like and how to cook it. Simple things like this can be revolutionary.

Blackberry-picking may have been immortalised in Seamus Heaney's poem of the same name, but the activity gained new traction a number of years ago when the Twelve Hotel in Barna, Co. Galway had the ingenious idea to offer children a free pizza for every kilo of blackberries dropped in to the hotel. Though not expecting a deluge, they certainly got more than they anticipated, with children lined up with buckets of blackberries waiting for their pizza.

Blackberry and apple pie, blackberry jam, blackberry and beetroot chutney and many other foodstuffs can be mustered up with a bucket of blackberries. You can even try blackberry wine from Móinéir Irish Wines, who are based in Co. Wicklow. They also make a strawberry wine and a raspberry wine. Blackberry wine pairs beautifully with venison, while the other two are great with Irish farmhouse cheese.

For an 18th-century Irish chutney, sweat some onions and garlic, then add a few handfuls of diced beetroot. At this point you can also add spices such as cinnamon or ginger. Cover with equal parts red wine, red wine vinegar and sugar. Simmer until the beetroot is soft, then fold in some blackberries. Season with salt and pack into sterilised jars. They're great for gifts. Giving the gift of something you have cooked, especially when it has some wild ingredients in it, is one of the greatest gifts you can give. It carries in it a piece of you and a piece of the landscape from which it came.

For Annette Sweeney in Donegal, blackberries were the one thing that she foraged as a child:

> Picking blackberries was an annual activity, though very few made it home to the kitchen. We made jam and jelly from them (recipes used were from *All in the Cooking*). I think the fact that the Gaelic textbooks at the time in Junior and Senior Infants told stories about *ag baint sméara dubha* [picking blackberries] added to the role they played in our lives each August/September. To this day, that memory comes to life in August as I continue to pick, preserve and enjoy them.

Elderberries

In the past, the elder tree was a symbol of anxiety for many farmers and country folk. Many Irish people claim that Judas hung himself from an elder tree (it was most likely a fig or olive tree) and that if you cut one down, the fairies will come and get you. When driving through Ireland, you will often see an elder tree standing firmly in the middle of a field because the farmer or landowner would have refused to cut it down.

Both the elder tree and the elderberry have a long history of medicinal use in Ireland. In her book *Ancient Cures, Charms, and Usages of Ireland: Contributions to Irish Lore*, Lady Wilde (1890) (Oscar's mother) detailed the many curative aspects of the tree, from treating epilepsy to alleviating burns.

Elderberry wine has long been a thing in Ireland, both as an alcoholic drink and as a medicine for pain. In their classic book on Irish foraging and folklore, *Wild and Free: Cooking from Nature*, Cyril and Kit Ó Céirín (1978) include elderberry recipes for soup, syrups, wine, jams and jellies. Dried elderberries were often used as a substitute for raisins in barmbrack. They also make a great addition to a sauce for game, such as wild duck, pigeon, pheasant and venison. Elderberries aren't good for your stomach if eaten raw, so always cook them, even if it's only a little.

Elderberries are a great marker of time and represent a true taste of an early Irish autumn. Find yourself an elder tree and you'll have berries for life.

Elderflowers

Elderflowers – and the autumn equivalent, elderberries (see above) – have been a staple of the Irish wild food calendar for centuries. Recipe books from the 17th century contain recipes for pickles, cordials and wine (a type of Irish 'champagne') made from the flowers, but I can well imagine them being used long before that, especially for medicinal purposes during the Middle Ages. Though the berries seem to have been held in more curative esteem, the flowers, distilled in water or in wax and almond oil, were used for skin conditions in the past.

May is one of my favourite months for foraging in Ireland. Over the years, you accumulate places where you know the flowers grow – by ruins of houses, near the racecourse, in the hedgerows of in Co. Clare. It's always nice to return to these places and see that the flowers are in bloom. It's another way of marking time.

As those large corymbs ripen, the cream-coloured flowers give off a honeyed, floral odour that perfumes the air with the first scent of summer. A year has passed but the new flowers give the appearance of sameness: the sweet smell of heavily scented elderflowers and the beginning of a new Irish summer.

Pickled elderflowers work with everything from goat cheese and monkfish to braised carrots and roast pork. The beauty is in their floral acidity. I prefer them to lemons or lime. An added bonus is that the brine you are left with can be used as an elderflower vinegar to season oysters and other shellfish.

To make pickled elderflowers, put 300ml white wine vinegar, 200ml water and 100g caster sugar in a saucepan and bring to a boil. Take 10 bunches of elderflowers and look them over to make sure there are no insects hiding in them. Put the bunches in a heatproof plastic container and pour the boiling pickling liquid over the flowers. Leave for a week in a cold, dark place (or in the fridge). Use the pickled flowers to add acidity to salads and use the remaining vinegar in dressings.

Another common way of using elderflowers in Ireland was making fritters from the smaller heads of the flowers and flavouring pancakes. Cyril and Kit Ó Céirín (1978) include an elderflower and gooseberry jam in *Wild and Free: Cooking from Nature*.

Fraughans

Bilberries are wild blueberries. In Ireland, they are called fraughans. They grow wild in acidic soil and can be found in many mountain ranges here, and are a good source of vitamin C.

They were traditionally picked in August, around the feast of Lughnasa to celebrate the harvest season. In her book *Irish Traditional Cooking* (1995), Darina Allen writes of Fraughan Sunday, the first Sunday in August, when the whole community would partake in gathering the berries.

Playwright Brian Friel memorialised them in his play *Dancing at Lughnasa* (1990). When the character Rose returns to the house having been away with Danny Bradley, she 'takes a fistful of berries and thrusts the fistful into her mouth. Then she wipes her mouth with her sleeve and the back of her hand. As she chews, she looks at her stained fingers.' As Fintan O'Toole observes, 'It is a brilliant image of sexuality and wildness and disturbance' (O'Toole 2013). Who knew wild berries could be so bold?

One of the nicest ways to eat them is to sprinkle them with sugar and serve with whipped cream. Using fraughans in cakes, pies and tarts was popular in the past. Jelly can also be made from bilberries. In Aniar, we preserve them in sugar syrup and keep them for the winter or make a flavoured liqueur using the berry and gin.

Meadowsweet

Meadowsweet, or queen of the meadow, is a member of the rose family that grows all over Ireland. Its creamy white flowers dominate the hedgerows between June and September. The druids considered it to be a sacred herb and it was used in ceremonies. In the Middle Ages, the herb was used to flavour beer in Ireland. Its name derives from being used to perfume the honeyed alcoholic drink mead, hence its Anglo-Saxon equivalent name: mead-sweetener.

This wild herb characterises the late summer months in Ireland. In Aniar we use the flowers mainly for dessert, first drying them and then sifting them to a fine powder that we use to flavour ice cream, sorbets and jellies. Mixing the powder with sugar makes a good flavouring for sweet pastries and cakes, lending them a decidedly floral character. You can also use the leaves and stalks to produce a vinegar by infusing them in apple cider vinegar. Lastly, an oil can made by blending the dried flowers with a neutral rapeseed oil and then gently heating it.

Alongside woodruff (see page 206), meadowsweet is perhaps the most important 'spice' that we use for desserts in Aniar. It represents a true taste of what I call new Irish cuisine (McMahon 2022).

Nettles

Along with oysters, seaweed and watercress, nettles are one of the central historic foods of Ireland. Yet our gradual retreat from nature and the natural world has made us wary of many wild things. Take nettles, for example. When was the last time you ate a nettle, if ever?

Nettles have a rich practical and mythological significance in Irish cooking. As well as being a nutritious food, they were also used for making cloth ever since the Bronze Age. There are a number of folk remedies that include nettles and many Irish customs associated with nettles. One, from Galway, involves drinking the juice of freshly pressed nettles to give you strength for the year ahead. Eating nettles is good for blood circulation.

Nettles abound around towns, in particular among waste grounds; indeed, sometimes they are hard *not* to encounter. Because of this, nettles are seen as a symbol of desolation in many Irish myths. Their ubiquity has aligned them with poverty and rejection in terms of Irish culinary modernism.

Nettle soup has a long history in Ireland, dating back to at least the 8th century in terms of written records. We can presume it had been a foodstuff in the preceding centuries too. The 8th-century monk St Colmcille reportedly lived off nettle soup.

The best time to pick nettles is in the spring and summer, before they flower. In Irish, small spring nettles are called *neanntóga*. Use the small leaves to make a wonderfully rich green purée or blanch them and add them to salads. Nettles can also be added to porridge, as Samuel Pepys observed in his diary in 1661. Beer and wine can be made with nettles and have been in the past (Ó Céirín and Ó Céirín 1978). Before the advent of cultivated cabbage, nettles were added to colcannon or champ along with other greens. According to Cyril and Cit Ó Céirín (1978: 126), boiled chicken and nettle broth (along with other greens such as wild garlic or leeks as well as oatmeal) was a typical dish in the North of Ireland and Scotland in the past.

Roses

Roses have a long history in cooking as an aromatic, and their associations inspire tales of love and lore. The Persians used rose petals to make wine, the Iranians to make jam and the English to flavour butter, so we can assume they were used in Ireland as well.

Many wild rose varieties abound in Ireland. This is due to the ways in which they breed, producing ever more selections. The native rose produces a small rosehip, which was traditionally used in medicine.

Rose petals evoke the emergence of the summer sun in Ireland and appear from May onwards. There are many different-coloured flowers, but the pink-red flowers of the Japanese rosehip are the most aromatic.

In cooking, roses contribute subtle, sweet-smelling notes, though for some people they just taste like Turkish Delight. In Aniar, we like to pickle the petals to make a rose vinegar. To do this, pick and wash a large handful of unsprayed red or pink rose petals. Gently warm some white wine vinegar or cider vinegar. Put the petals in a Kilner jar and pour the cooled vinegar over them. Leave to infuse for a few days at room temperature, then place in the fridge. You can also make rose sugar syrup or dry them and use them as a powder over chocolates and fudge.

Along with oysters, seaweed and watercress, nettles are one of the central historic foods of Ireland. Yet our gradual retreat from nature and the nautral world has made us wary of many wild things. Take nettles, for example. When was the last time you ate a nettle, if ever?

Three-cornered leeks

According to British forager Miles Irving, three-cornered leeks (also called three-cornered garlic) have been cultivated in the British Isles since 1759. Following cultivation, they quickly colonised much of the verges, edges and banks of roads and fields and now populate roadside verges all around Ireland. From March to May they produce a wonderful little white flower that emits a deep garlic smell when pressed to the nose.

When picking them in the past, my morally conscious daughter used to tell me to stop stealing them. She used to think that I would just reverse into someone's driveway and get out to invade their garden. You see, many people have three-cornered leeks in their garden but mistake them for white-flowered bluebells. If in doubt, smell them. These guys are unmistakable. Two hundred years ago in Ireland, it was said that peasants hung three-cornered leeks outside their door to keep vampires away.

From soup to pesto and flavoured oil, these little leeks are great for getting you out into your local landscape. As well as using the flowers in a spring salad, the flowers also pair well with shellfish. You can use the leaves of this plant in a similar way to chives, though use them sparingly because their flavour is more robust. Both the flowers and the stems work well with lightly grilled oysters. To take the garlicky edge off the stems, quickly blanch them in boiling water and refresh in ice water. Finely chop and fold into room-temperature butter. Put a little knob of butter on top of a native oyster and grill just until it melts, being careful not to overcook the oyster. A potato and three-cornered leek soup should keep any cold at bay. Finally, I fold them into potato bread when we make it in Aniar.

Wild garlic

Wild garlic was 'an extremely important food in ancient Ireland (Jackson 2014: 169). It has been eaten here for thousands of years. It grows in woodlands all over the island. While its green leaves pop through the moist soil in early spring, it's not until late spring that their white flower blossoms can be seen in full bloom, which is when the air surrounding them fills with a garlic-like scent.

It's hard to go wrong with wild garlic because of its distinct smell and ease of identification. Its pungent aroma hits you as you walk into any wood where it grows.

In the Middle Ages, wild garlic was used to flavour bread, butter, broths and stews (Rutty 1772). It was also recommended for colds, coughs and asthma. Nowadays, the flowers are wonderful sprinkled over salads, while their tiny white tendrils offset luscious green soups beautifully. In the 19th century, according to Nicolas Williams, the leaves were used to wrap butter in order to help preserve and flavour it (cited in Jackson 2014: 169).

Wild garlic has different stages as it grows through the season. In early spring I eat it raw, straight out of the ground. Its tiny tips taste outstanding. As it grows larger, the leaves can be used to make a wild garlic champ or a wild garlic pesto made with hazelnuts and extra-virgin rapeseed oil. Making your own is easy. Take a large handful of freshly foraged wild garlic. Pick through it for small insects (unless you require additional protein!), rinse briefly and pat dry. Put in a blender and cover with extra-virgin Irish rapeseed oil. Add a handful of toasted hazelnuts and some diced Hegarty's Cheddar (or another hard Irish cheese). Season with sea salt and blend until smooth. If you want the pesto to be thicker, add more wild garlic leaves. Pour the pesto into a clean glass jar, seal and keep in the fridge. In recent years, wild garlic pesto has appeared all over the country at artisan markets. It's a wonderful alternative to the dull, lifeless jars of basil pesto one encounters everywhere.

The seed heads of wild garlic can be preserved and used as a little Irish caper. To do this, wait until the final flowers have fallen, then collect as many seed heads as possible. Snip the tiny seed heads away from the stem. Put them in a clean jar and lightly salt them. Seal the jar and leave it in the fridge for a week. Remove the seed heads, rinse and dry, then cover completely in a light vinegar. Then the waiting begins. In Aniar, we usually use ours in the autumn. These little pickled buds pair wonderfully with wild game. These are probably my favourite Irish food – they are Irish 'gold.'

Wild mushrooms

There is a long tradition of picking field mushrooms in Ireland. Field mushrooms are also called horse mushrooms, as they usually grow where a large number of horses are kept. These mushrooms would often be simply fried in butter and herbs. In *Wild and Free: Cooking from Nature*, Cyril and Kit Ó Céirín (1978: 122) observe that a relish would sometimes be made with field mushrooms: chopped mushrooms and salt would be left to break down in a glass jar until a 'thick black relish' formed. Onions and black pepper were often added later, and it would be cooked. This process is not a million miles away from making mushroom ketchup, albeit without the sugar and spices. We make something similar in Aniar but only keep the liquid. We call it mushroom 'soy' and use it pretty much as you would use regular soy sauce for seasoning vegetarian and vegan dishes.

Theodora FitzGibbon writes that a soup would be made from field mushrooms. In old manuscript books they are spelled 'musharooms' and this cry, FitzGibbon writes, would be heard 'by the sellers in Dublin's Moore Street market' (1983: 23). In her book *The Farm by Lough Gur*, Mary Carbery (2017) writes of Sissy O'Brien picking 'the earliest mountain mushrooms' for the Countess de Salis.

It still confounds me why we don't have a stronger relationship with the myriad of other wild mushrooms that we now use regularly in Aniar. Was it a question of land, perhaps? A legacy of colonialism and the Famine? In truth, the legacy of this time on our food culture still has not been adequately assessed.

Or perhaps we did and there just aren't any written records? Hedgehog mushrooms, yellow chanterelles, girolles, birch bolete, morels, cauliflower fungus, oyster mushrooms, ceps (aka porcini; also called penny buns in Ireland and the UK) and truffles are among some of the mushrooms that we use in the restaurant today, all of which hail from the island of Ireland. While our interest in wild mushrooms may have increased with the influx of Italian and Polish people into Ireland since the late 1990s and early 2000s, FitzGibbon does mention the use of both 'apricot coloured' chanterelles and a 'delicious fungus commonly called Jew's ear' (now called wood ear) that would be dried and used to make a 'Chinese-Irish stew' (FitzGibbon 1968: 163).

I find it difficult to believe that the Celtic peoples who arrived in Ireland, as well as the Vikings, did not partake of these wonderful culinary delights. Indeed, we could go back even further to the Neolithic and even the Mesolithic ages, to hunter-gatherers who 'had a potentially plant-rich diet supplemented by fungi' (McClean 1993: 2).

The golden chanterelle is the superior wild Irish mushroom, in my opinion. This unique yellowish, resplendent mushroom pops its head up through woodland foliage and under hardwood trees such as oak, maple, white pine, poplar and birch. Chanterelles form a symbiotic relationship with the roots of these trees.

Wood sorrel

Wood sorrel is one of my favourite wild plants, whether in a salad or eaten by itself. The intense lemony flavour of the leaf makes it a wonderful substitute for lemons with fish dishes or anything else requiring a gentle acidity. Wood sorrel also works well with desserts to help balance fat and sweetness. Try it with poached pink rhubarb and honey-sweetened cream for a delicate taste of new Irish cuisine (McMahon 2022).

Because of its small size, wood sorrel is not suitable to use in soups or hot dishes. Common or sheep's sorrel is much better because they are bigger and hardier.

Wood sorrel gets several mentions in old Irish literature, particularly in the medieval Irish text *Buile Suibhne* (*The Madness of Suibhne*), which Seamus Heaney translated into the modern poem 'Sweeney Astray' (Heaney 1998: 191–2). Adrift in the wild, the king feeds on wood sorrel to quell his hunger:

> *It is nature's pantry*
> *with its sorrels, its wood sorrels,*
> *its berries, its wild garlic.*
> *its black sloes and its brown acorns.*
> *The madmen would beat each other for the pick of its*
> *   watercresses and for the beds on its banks.*

Wood sorrel is supposed to be the original shamrock that St Patrick used to explain the holy trinity to the pagan Irish, though this is questionable due to the absence of any concrete evidence. In Irish folk medicine, wood sorrel was used to alleviate stomach and digestive aliments.

Woodruff

It is difficult to ascertain what vegetables and plants the first settlers to Ireland picked and ate, but I like to imagine my ancient Irish ancestors sitting around the campfire drinking a cup of woodruff tea. It may seem a little fanciful, but I don't think we give our ancient ancestors enough credit. I think they had a sophisticated understanding of nature and moved according to the seasons (Warren 2015). All edible herbs and plants would have provided nutrition.

Woodruff is a small upright plant with sweetly scented flowers that grows in forests. Because of its sweet-smelling nature, the herb was used to sweeten homes. It was strewn on floors, stuffed into pillows and placed between sheets.

Alongside meadowsweet, it's one of the key flavours we use in Aniar for pastry. It's beautiful dried and used in both savoury and sweet ways. When dried, the herb has a faint almond scent and often reminds me of marzipan. In late spring, its flowers can be picked and used to decorate tarts and desserts. They are nice pickled because they give off a hint of vanilla. Because of its woodland location, I like to pair it with game in the autumn, adding it to sauces for venison and wild duck.

If I had to pick just two wild herbs that are vital to the flavours of Aniar, woodruff and meadowsweet would be the two that impart the specific aromas of what I call new Irish cuisine (McMahon 2022). For me, new Irish cuisine is another part of the Irish food story that looks at how we can use our wild indigenous plants and seaweeds to engender a cuisine of our own.

100

Yellowman

Yellowman, or 'yallaman', was traditionally found at stalls at country fairs. It's usually associated with Northern Ireland, particularly the Ould Lammas Fair in Ballycastle, Co. Antrim, one of the oldest continuous fairs in Northern Ireland. It is a decidedly sweet toffee-like treat and was often sold with dillisk (dulse). A folk ballad written by John Henry MacAuley mentions the peculiar pairings:

> At the auld Lammas Fair, were you ever there?
> Were you ever at the fair of Ballycastle, oh?
> Did you treat your Mary Anne to some dulse and yallaman
> At the auld Lammas Fair of Ballycastle, oh?

Yellowman is similar to honeycomb, though denser, with the texture of toffee. Its bright yellow colour also distinguishes it from honeycomb. It was traditionally given by a boy to a girl when they were dating (Mahon 1991: 48).

Yellowman is said to be a feature of the cuisine of Northern Ireland, along with Veda bread, dulse, Ardglass potted herring, fifteens, farls and the Ulster fry.

Conclusion

In the play *Making History* by the late Donegal playwright Brian Friel, the character of Hugh O'Donnell speaks of the awful impact that the Nine Years' War (1594–1603) had on the province of Ulster: 'Everywhere are people scavenging in the fields, hoking up bits of roots, eating fistfuls of watercress. They look like skeletons' (Friel 1989: 43).

While Friel's description draws on the actual account of the Munster wars of the 1570s by the English poet Edmund Spenser in his work *A View of the Present State of Ireland* (1897), it shows the effect of the scorched earth policy of the English. These periods of deliberate famine and starvation had a long and traumatic impact on the people of Ireland in relation to food, both in terms of its production and its consumption, from the 16th to the 20th century. It also impacted our ability to tell our own food story.

Yet this is just one aspect of the Irish food story. Over the course of my own and others' research, I have realised that there are a multitude of other moments that we can also draw from to narrate the food culture of the island.

In some ways, we were blinded by independence to believe that there was only one 'story' on the island of Ireland. For example, the Big House tradition that is so often scorned as being colonial and 'not Irish' must also be folded into the Irish food experience. A Dublin recipe from 1778 for wild duck cooked in port demonstrates the duality of this position. An indigenous foodstuff meets a foreign aspect of another cuisine and thus another layer is added to the experience of food in Ireland.

This is just one example. There are many others, from the sea bass eaten by the first settlers over 10,000 years ago to the Celtic and Viking people who brought different European and Nordic traditions to this island. Food is always in flux. This is why I have used the indefinite article to preface the 'Irish food story' of this book. There are many Irish food stories, both written and unwritten. Food makes and unmakes us continually.

There are many
Irish food stories,
both written and
unwritten. Food
makes and unmakes
us continually.

Bibliography

Allen, Darina, *Irish Traditional Cooking: Recipes from Ireland's Heritage* (Gill & Macmillan, 1995) (revised edition 2012).

— *Forgotten Skills of Cooking: 700 Recipes Showing You Why the Time-honoured Ways Are the Best* (Kyle Cathie, 2009).

Allen, Myrtle, *The Ballymaloe Cookbook* (Gill & Macmillan, 1984) (first pub. 1977).

— *Cooking at Ballymaloe House* (Stewart, Tabori & Chang, 2000).

Andrews, Colman, *The Country Cooking of Ireland* (Chronicle Books, 2009).

Anonymous, *Two New and Curious Essays … And a Discourse Concerning Ways of Preparing and Dressing Potatoes for the Table* (1732).

Armstrong, Alison, *The Joyce of Cooking* (Station Hill Press, 1986).

Bardon, Jonathan, *A History of Ireland in 250 Episodes* (Gill & Macmillan, 2008).

Barthes, Roland, 'Toward a Psychosociology of Contemporary Food Consumption' in Carole Counihan and Penny Van Esterik (eds.), *Food and Culture: A Reader,* 3rd edition (Routledge, 1997), 28–35.

Beckett, Samuel, *Company* (Calder, 1980).

Bowen, Elizabeth, *The Little Girls* (Johnathan Cape, 1964).

Boyle, Judith, 'A Short History of Irish Poitín', *RTÉ Brainstorm* [website], 20 June 2023.

Brent, Harry, 'Ireland's Favourite Deli Food Has Been Revealed – and It's Hardly a Surprise', *Irish Post*, 8 October 2020.

Brown, Terence, *Ireland: A Social and Cultural History 1922–2002* (Harper Perennial, 2004).

Buckley, Gavin et al., 'An Investigation into Caffeine Consumption and Self-Reported Dependency in the Republic of Ireland', *International Undergraduate Journal of Health Sciences,* 1/2 (2021).

Campion, Edmund, *A History of Ireland Written in the Year 1571* (Gayley Press, 2009).

Carbery, Mary, *The Farm by Lough Gur* (Lilliput Press, 2017) (first pub. 1937).

Cashman, Dorothy, 'Ireland's Culinary Manuscripts' in Darina Allen, *Irish Traditional Cooking: Recipes from Ireland's Heritage* (Gill & Macmillan, 2012), 14–15.

— 'An Investigation of Irish Culinary History through Manuscript Cookbooks, with Particular Reference to the Gentry of County Kilkenny (1714–1830)', PhD thesis (TUDublin, 2016).

— and Farrelly, John, '"Is Irish Stew the Only Kind of Stew We Can Afford to Make, Mother?": The History of a Recipe', *Folk Life*, 59/2 (2021), 81–100.

Chadbourne, K., 'The Knife Against the Wave: Fairies, Fishermen, and the Sea', *Béaloideas*, 80 (2012), 70–85.

Civitello, Linda, *Cuisine and Culture: A History of Food and People* (Wiley, 2004).

Claiborne, Craig, *The New York Times Food Encyclopedia* (New York Times, 1985).

Clarkson, L.A. and Crawford, Margaret E. (eds.), *Feast and Famine: Food and Nutrition in Ireland 1500–1920* (Oxford University Press, 2001).

Connery, Clare, *In an Irish Country Kitchen* (Simon & Schuster, 1993).

Creedon, John, *An Irish Folklore Treasury* (Gill Books, 2022).

Crow, Hugh, *Memoirs of the Late Captain Hugh Crow of Liverpool* (Longman, Rees, Orme, Brown & Green, 1830).

Cullen, Louis M., *The Emergence of Modern Ireland 1600–1900* (Batsford, 1981).

— 'Comparative Aspects of the Irish Diet, 1550–1850' in Hans J. Teuteberg (ed.), *European Food History: A Research Review* (Leicester University Press, 1991).

Danaher, Kevin, *In Ireland Long Ago* (Mercier Press, 1962).

De Casteau, Lancelot, *Ouverture de Cuisine* (Leonard Streel, 1604).

Dennison, Polly, 'Dublin is the Second-most "Coffee-obsessed" Capital in the World', *Irish Times*, 14 July 2021.

Department of Agriculture, *Cookery Notes* (Dublin: Government Publications, 1924).

Digby, Marie Claire, 'Spice Bag: How to Make Ireland's Favourite Takeaway Dish at Home', *Irish Times*, 7 December 2021.

Dunton, John, *Teague Land: Or a Merry Ramble to the Wild Irish* (Four Courts Press, 2003) (first pub. 1698).

Evans, E. Estyn, *Irish Heritage* (Dundalgan Press, 1942).

FitzGibbon, Theodora, *A Taste of Ireland* (Houghton Mifflin Company, 1968).

— *The Food of the Western World* (Hutchinson, 1976).

— *Irish Traditional Food* (Gill & Macmillan, 1983).

Fitzpatrick, Elizabeth and Kelly, James (eds.), *Food and Drink in Ireland* (Royal Irish Academy, 2016).

Friel, Brian, *Making History* (Faber & Faber, 1989).

— *Dancing at Lughnasa* (Faber & Faber, 1990).

Garmey, Jane, *Great British Cooking: A Well-kept Secret* (Harper Collins, 1981).

Gilligan, Nikolah, 'Salt from Seaweed? An Experimental Archaeology Perspective on Salt in Early Medieval Ireland', *Feast*, 2 (February 2020). feastjournal.co.uk/issue/salt

Giraldus Cambrensis (Gerald of Wales), *The Topography of Ireland*, translated by Thomas Forester with additional notes by Thomas Wright (In Parentheses Publications, 2000).

Greenwood, Vanessa, 'Simple Swiss Roll: A Recipe for an Old Favourite', *Irish Times*, 17 February 2018.

Hartley, Dorothy, *Irish Holiday* (R.M. McBride, 1939).

Hartley, L.P., *The Go-Between* (Hamish Hamilton, 1953).

Hayward, Stephen, 'Iconic Food Firm to Be Frozen Out of Supermarkets as Brand Is Dropped', *Daily Mirror*, 20 January 2016.

Heaney, Seamus, *Opened Ground: Poems 1966–1996* (Faber & Faber, 1998).

Hennessy, Caroline and Jensen, Kristin, *Sláinte: The Complete Guide to Irish Craft Beer and Cider* (New Island, 2014).

Hickey, Margaret, *Ireland's Green Larder* (Unbound, 2018).

Horgan-Jones, Jack, 'Superquinn Sausages: Butcher Recalls Invention of Popular Pork Product', *Irish Times*, 25 April 2019.

Houlihan, Barry, 'A Short History of Irish Coffee', *RTÉ Brainstorm* [website], 22 September 2023.

Irwin, Florence, *The Cookin' Woman: Irish Country Recipes* (Blackstaff Press, 1949). First printed as *Irish Country Recipes* (The Northern Whig, 1937) (repr. 1994).

Joyce, James, *Dubliners* (Penguin, 2000) (first pub. 1914).

— *Ulysses* (Shakespeare & Co., 1922).

Keane, John, 'The Word for "Seaweed" Has Far Richer Meaning in the Irish Language', *Irish Independent*, 28 October 2021.

Keane, John B., *Strong Tea* (Mercier Press, 1963).

Keegan, Clare, *Small Things Like These* (Faber & Faber, 2021).

Kelly, Fergus, *Early Irish Farming: A Study Based Mainly on the Law-Tract of the 7th and 8th Centuries AD* (Dublin Institute for Advanced Studies, 1997).

Kickham, Charles J., *Knocknagow* (James Duffy, 1879). exclassics.com/knockngw/knconts.htm

Kitchiner, William, *The Cook's Oracle* (A. Constable & Company, 1822).

Lamb, J.G. and Hayes, A., *The Irish Apple: History and Myth* (Irish Seed Savers Association, 2012).

Laverty, Maura, *Never No More* (Virago Press, 2004) (first pub. 1942).

— *Kind Cooking* (The Kerryman, 1955).

— *Full and Plenty: Traditional Irish Cookbook* (The Irish Flour Millers' Press, 1986) (first pub. 1960).

Lees, Frederic Richard, *The Condensed Argument for the Legislative Prohibition of the Liquor Traffic* (J. Caudwell, 1864).

Lovell, M.S., *The Edible Mollusca of Great Britain and Ireland* (L. Reeve & Co., 1867).

Lucas, A.T., 'Irish Food before the Potato', *Gwerin: A Half-yearly Journal of Folk Life*, 3/2 (1960), 8–43.

— *Irish-Norse Relations: Time for a Reappraisal* (Cork, 1966).

— (ed.), *Cattle in Ancient Ireland* (Boethius Press, 1989).

Mac Con Iomaire, Máirtín, 'The History of Seafood in Irish Cuisine and Culture', *Proceedings of the Oxford Symposium on Food and Cookery* (Prospect Books, 2005), 219–33.

— 'Exploring the "Food Motif" in Songs from the Irish Tradition', Dublin Gastronomy Symposium, 3 June 2014.

— 'Recognizing Food as Part of Ireland's Intangible Culture', *Folk Life: Journal of Ethnological Studies*, 56/2 (2018).

— and Cashman, Dorothy, 'Irish Culinary Manuscripts and Printed Cookbooks: A Discussion', *Petits Propos Culinaires*, 94 (2011), 81–101.

— and Maher, Eamon (eds.), *Tickling the Palate: Gastronomy in Irish Literature and Culture* (Peter Lang, 2014).

— and Óg Gallagher, Pádraic, 'The Potato in Irish Cuisine and Culture', *Journal of Culinary Science & Technology*, 7/2–3 (2009), 152–67.

— — , 'Irish Corned Beef: A Culinary History', *Journal of Culinary Science & Technology*, 9/1 (2011), 27–43.

Mac Thomáis, Éamonn, *Gur Cake and Coal Blocks* (O'Brien Press, 1976).

Magan, Manchán, *Thirty-two Words for Field: Lost Words of the Irish Landscape* (Gill, 2020).

Mahon, Bríd, *Land of Milk and Honey* (Poolbeg Press, 1991).

Mallory, J.P., *The Origins of the Irish* (Thames & Hudson, 2015) (first pub. 2013).

Markham, Gervase, *The English Huswife* (Roger Jackson, 1615).

Martin, M., *A Description of the Western Islands of Scotland* (Andrew Bell, 1703).

McClatchie, M. et al., 'Neolithic Farming in North-western Europe: Archaeobotanical Evidence from Ireland', *Journal of Archaeological Science*, 51 (2014), 206–15.

McClean, R., 'Eat Your Greens: An Examination of the Potential Diet Available in Ireland during the Mesolithic', *Ulster Journal of Archaeology*, 56 (1993), 1–8.

McDonald, Brian, 'Top Breakfast Baguette Rolls into Irish History', *Irish Independent*, 12 May 2008.

McDonald, Frank, 'Jammet's: A Dublin Treasure Crowded with Gourmets and Wits', *Irish Times*, 14 May 2014.

McGee, Harold, *McGee on Food and Cooking: An Encyclopaedia of Kitchen Science, History and Culture* (Hodder & Stoughton, 2004) (first pub. 1984).

McMahon, Jp, *The Irish Cookbook* (Phaidon, 2020).

— *An Alphabet of Aniar: Notes for a New Irish Cuisine* (Godot Press, 2022).

Medcalf, Patricia, 'Guinness and Food: Ingredients in an Unlikely Gastronomic Revolution', Dublin Gastronomy Symposium (2016).

Melroe, Eliza, *An Economical and New Method of Cookery; Describing Upwards of Eighty Cheap, Wholesome, and Nourishing Dishes* (London: Printed and published for the author, 1798).

Millar McCowan, 'Millar McCowan History', https://web.archive.org/web/20110714094943/ http:/www.millar-mccowan.com/company/history.html.

Miller, Ian, 'Nutritional Decline in Post-Famine Ireland c. 1851–1922', *Proceedings of the Royal Irish Academy: Archaeology, Celtic Studies, History, Literature*, 115C (2015), 307–24.

Moran, D.P., *The Philosophy of Irish Ireland* (UCD Press, 2006) (first pub. 1905).

Moryson, Feynes, *An Itinerary: Containing His Ten Years Travel Through the Twelve Dominions of Germany, Bohemia, Switzerland, Netherland, Denmark, Poland, Italy, Turkey, France, England, Scotland and Ireland* (1617). archive.org/details/fynesmorysons04moryuoft

National Folklore Collection, The Schools' Collection, Volume 0528, Page 080, UCD. duchas.ie/en/cbes/4922112/4853217/4949898

New-York Tribune, 'Chicken à la King', 7 March 1915.

Noonan, Aoife, 'This Large Slice of Baked Nostalgia Won't Let You Down', *Irish Times*, 13 November 2021.

O'Casey, Seán, *Autobiographies 1* (Macmillan, 1980a) (first pub. 1963).

— *Autobiographies 2* (Macmillan, 1980b) (first pub. 1963). Ó Céirín, Cyril and Ó Céirín, Kit, *Wild and Free: Cooking from Nature* (O'Brien Press, 1978).

Ó Conghaile, Pól, 'Crisp Sandwiches: Demand Sky-High for New Aer Lingus Snack', *Irish Independent*, 16 June 2015.

Ó Crohan, Tomás, *The Islander* (*An t-Oileánach*) (Gill Books, 2013) (first pub. 1929).

O'Mara, Jane Veronica and O'Reilly, Fionnuala, *A Trifle, A Coddle, A Fry: An Irish Literary Cookbook* (Moyer Bell, 1993).

Ó Muirithe, Diarmuid, *Words We Don't Use (Much Anymore)* (Gill Books, 2011).

O'Toole, Fintan, 'Culture Shock: A History of Irish Drama in 10 Foods', *Irish Times*, 23 November 2013.

— *We Don't Know Ourselves: A Personal History of Ireland Since 1958* (Apollo, 2022*a*).

— 'The Old Irish Way of Doing Things Must Become Extinct – Or Else We Will', *Irish Times*, 2 August 2022*b*.

Ohlmeyer, Jane, *Making Empire: Ireland, Imperialism and the Early Modern World* (Oxford, 2023).

Pellechia, Thomas, *Wine: The 8,000-Year-Old Story of the Wine Trade* (Running Press, 2006).

Pococke, Richard, *Pococke's Tour of Ireland in 1752*, ed. George T. Stokes (Hodges Figgis, 1891).

Pope, Conor, 'Ireland's Favourite Dinners Revealed – and They're Not Quite What You'd Expect', *Irish Times*, 5 February 2020.

Power, P., 'On a Find of Ancient Jars in Cork City', *Journal of the Cork Historical and Archaeological Society*, 33/10–11 (1928).

Preston-Matto, Lahney (trans.), *Aislinge Meic Conglinne: The Vision of MacConglinne* (Syracuse University Press, 2010).

Redmond, Caitríona, 'Why Gur Cake Needs EU Designated Status', *Irish Independent*, 10 April 2014.

Rhames, Aaron, *Instructions for Managing Bees (1733)* (Kessinger Publishing, 2009).

Rhatigan, Prannie, *Irish Seaweed Kitchen* (Booklink, 2009).

Rutty, John, *An Essay towards the Natural History of the County of Dublin* (W. Sleater, 1772).

Ryan, Kate, 'The Evolution of Corn in Irish Food Culture', *Scoop*, 1 (2022), 60–5.

Sayid, Ruki, 'Just Desserts! Angel Delight Voted Nation's Favourite Childhood Dish', *Daily Mirror*, 23 June 2015.

Scherer, Cordula, 'The Remarkable Ray of Dublin's Ringsend', *Arcadia*, 41 (Autumn 2020). https://doi.org/10.5282/rcc/9150

Sexton, Regina, *A Little History of Irish Food* (Kyle Books, 1998).

— 'Food and Culinary Cultures in Pre-Famine Ireland', *Proceedings of the Royal Irish Academy: Archaeology, Celtic Studies, History, Literature*, 115C (2015), 257–306.

— 'The Halloween Conundrum: Is It a Barm Brack or a Barn Brack?', *RTÉ Brainstorm* [website], 27 October 2023.

— and Cowan, Cathal, *Ireland's Traditional Foods: An Exploration of Irish Local and Typical Foods and Drinks* (Teagasc, 1997).

Sheridan, Monica, *Monica's Kitchen* (Dublin: Castle Publications, 1963).

— *The Art of Irish Cooking* (Gramercy, 1965).

Sibley, Fiona, 'Table Talk', *Guardian*, 11 November 2008.

Smith, Eliza, *The Compleat Housewife* (Andrews McMeel Publishing, 2012) (first pub. 1727).

Smyth, Jessica and Evershed, Richard P., 'The Molecules of Meat: New Insights into Neolithic Foodways', *Proceedings of the Royal Irish Academy: Archaeology, Celtic Studies, History, Literature*, 115C (2015), 27–46.

Somerville, Edith O. and Ross, Martin, *Some Experiences of an Irish RM* (Longmans, Green & Co., 1899).

Spenser, Edmund, 'A View to the Present State of Ireland', in *Complete Works of Edmund Spenser* (Macmillan & Co., 1897).

St John Gogarty, Oliver, *As I Was Going Down Sackville Street* (Rich & Cowan, 1937).

— *Tumbling in the Hay* (Sphere, 1982) (first pub. 1939).

Stevens, John, *The Journal of John Stevens: Containing a Brief Account of the War in Ireland, 1689–1691* (Clarendon Press, 1912).

Stevens, Patricia Bunning, *Rare Bits: Unusual Origins of Popular Recipes* (Ohio University Press, 1998).

Taylor, Alice, *Quench the Lamp* (St. Martin's Press, 1994).

Thackeray, William M., *The Irish Sketch Book* (Thomas Nelson & Sons, 1900) (first pub. 1843).

Truxes, T. M., *Irish-American Trade 1660–1783* (Cambridge University Press, 1988).

Valencia, Blanca, Laffan, Dee and Chin, Mei, *Soup* (Blasta Books, 2023).

Walker, J. C., *An Historical Essay on the Dress of the Ancient Irish/Memoir of the Armour and Weapons of the Irish* (Royal Irish Academy, 1788).

Walsh, Enda, *Disco Pigs and Sucking Dublin: Two Plays* (Nick Hern Books, 1997).

Warren, Graeme, ' "Mere Food Gatherers They, Parasites upon Nature…": Food and Drink in the Mesolithic Ireland', *Proceedings of the Royal Irish Academy: Archaeology, Celtic Studies, History, Literature*, 115C (2015), 1–26.

Went, Arthur E.J., 'The Ling in Irish Commerce', *The Journal of the Royal Society of Antiquaries of Ireland*, 78/2 (1948).

— 'Eel Fishing at Athlone: Past and Present', *The Journal of the Royal Society of Antiquaries of Ireland*, 80/2 (1950) 146–54.

Wilde, Lady Francesca Speranza, *Ancient Cures, Charms, and Usages of Ireland: Contributions to Irish Lore* (Ward & Downey, 1890).

Wilde, Oscar, *The Importance of Being Earnest and Other Plays* (Penguin, 1986).

Woodman, Peter, *Ireland's First Settlers: Time and the Mesolithic* (Oxbow Books, 2015).

Wyse Jackson, Peter, *Ireland's Generous Nature: The Past and Present Uses of Wild Plants in Ireland* (Missouri Botanical Garden Press, 2014).

Yenne, Bill, *Guinness: The 250-Year Quest for the Perfect Pint* (John Wiley & Sons, 2007).

Young, Arthur, *A Tour in Ireland: 1776–1779*, Vol. 76 (Cassell, 1887).

Index

Acknowledgements

I would like to thank the many minds that contributed to the formation of this book, from the authors who I cite and reference to the many others whose conversations contributed to the ideas in this book.

Thank you to my business partner, Drigín Gaffey, for your constant support and commitment over the years.

Thank you also to my parents, Carol and Gerard, for your undying faith in me, and to my brothers and sister, especially Edel, who has shared in my journey of Irish food from a designer's point of view.

Thank you to my children, Heather and Martha, for making sure I keep my feet on the ground.

Thank you to my partner, Aoife Qualter, for your love and support.

Thank you to my PA, Abigail Colleran, for your constant commitment to the Irish food story.

Thank you to all the staff at Aniar and Cava Bodega, past and present, who have made both restaurants their own and pursued the idea of Irish food and food in Ireland with constant determination, energy and creativity.

Thank you to the staff of Tartare Café and Wine Bar who showcased a new vision of what Irish food could be.

Thank you to Kristin Jensen for your editorial eye and for making the text better than it was to begin with and to Matt Cox for your wonderful design and the impeccable way you captured images for my words.

And thank you to John Ward, my dear friend and oyster producer, who passed away suddenly in June 2024. You taught me so much about oysters. Your passion for Irish food shall never be forgotten.

About the author

Jp McMahon is a Michelin-starred chef, restaurateur and the author of the best-selling *The Irish Cookbook*. He is an ambassador for Irish food, travelling widely to promote Ireland, its produce and its food culture.

Jp is also the founder of and host to one of the biggest and most talked-about international food events in Europe, Food on the Edge, that features the best chefs, food entrepreneurs and culinary minds from across the globe.

Jp is a member of Euro-Toques Ireland and is committed to the educational and ethical aspects of food, to buying and supporting the best of local and free-range produce, and to engaging directly with farmers and producers. He is also a regular contributor to RTÉ Radio One and Newstalk radio and has a monthly slot on RTÉ television. He wrote a weekly column for the *Irish Times* for eight years.

He has a PhD in Drama and Theatre from the University of Galway and is a practising playwright.

@mistereatgalway

Nine Bean Rows
23 Mountjoy Square
Dublin D01 E0F8
Ireland
@9beanrowsbooks
ninebeanrowsbooks.com

First published 2024
Text © Jp McMahon, 2024

ISBN: 978-1-7384795-0-4

Editor: Kristin Jensen
Designer: Matt Cox at Newman+Eastwood, newmanandeastwood.com
Indexer: Jane Rogers
Endpapers produced by: Nataliia Dragunova
Printed by L&C Printing Group, Poland

Cover photographs: iStockphoto (barley, bread, Dublin Bay prawn, oats), Shutterstock (hazelnuts, pig, potatoes, wild garlic)

The paper in this book is produced using pulp from managed forests.

10 9 8 7 6 5 4 3 2 1

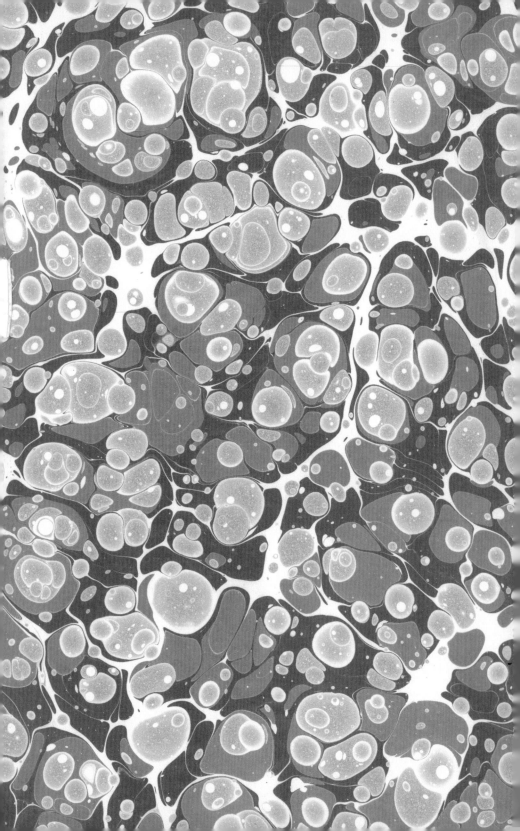